THE CHRONIC SCHIZOPHRENIAS

Dedicated to my daughters,
Inger Katharina and Anne Marie Ragna

THE CHRONIC SCHIZOPHRENIAS

by

Christian Astrup

Former Professor of Social Psychiatry
University of Tromsø
Tromsø, Norway

Docent, University of Oslo
Oslo, Norway

UNIVERSITETSFORLAGET
Oslo — Bergen — Tromsø

© THE NORWEGIAN RESEARCH COUNCIL FOR SCIENCE
AND THE HUMANITIES 1979
(Norges almenvitenskapelige forskningsråd)

Section: C.38.65-2T

ISBN 82-00-01810-5

Cover design: Per Syversen

Distribution offices:

NORWAY
Universitetsforlaget
Box 2977, Tøyen
Oslo 6

UNITED KINGDOM
Global Book Resources Ltd.
109 Great Russel Street
London WC 1B 3ND

UNITED STATES and CANADA
Columbia University Press
136 South Broadway
Irvington-on-Hudson
New York 10533

Printed in Norway by
Foto-Trykk, Trøgstad

GELEITWORT

Die chronischen Schizophrenien werden in der psychiatrischen Wissenschaft sehr vernachlässigt. Man meint vielfach, sie seien in der Beurteilung dessen, was man schizophren nennt, ohne Bedeutung, es komme nur auf die akuten Zustände an. Man täuscht sich darin sehr. In den akuten Zuständen verwischen sich die Grenzen, die zu ziehen sind. Die Feststellungen, die man trifft, werden dadurch unbestimmt, die Aussagen unverbindlich. In den chronischen Zuständen hat man dagegen Bilder vor sich, die eine feste Gestalt aufweisen. Sie zwingen zur Frage, was ihnen gemeinsam ist, was andererseits dafür spricht, dass keine Einheit "Schizophrenie" vorliegt, sondern eine "Gruppe von Schizophrenien", von der schon Eugen Bleuler einst Sprach. Von hier, nicht von den akuten Zuständen aus, wird man einer Lösung der Frage näher kommen, was der Krankheit zugrundeliegt. Bisher weiss man darüber ja trotz aller Bemühungen sehr wenig. Ein zweiter Grund für eine wissenschaftliche Abneigung gegenüber den chronischen Schizophrenen rührt daher, dass man glaubte, hier Fälle vor sich zu haben, bei denen man therapeutisch nichts mehr tun könne. Hier ist deutlich ein Wandel eingetreten, seit man "Endzustände" nicht mehr für unabänderlich hält, sondern mit soziotherapeutischen Massnahmen so viel zum Wohle der Kranken tun kann.

Es ist ein grosses Verdienst von Astrup, dass er sich in umfassender Weise der chronischen Schizophrenen angenommen hat. Er untersuchte einerseits die Symptombilder, durch die sie sich unterscheiden, er rückte andererseits die Schwere der Erkrankung in den Vordergrund und kam, indem er beide Gesichtspunkte verband, zu neuartigen und wesentlichen Feststellungen. Von besonderem Interesse ist in diesem Zusammenhang seine Bestätigung, dass schwere Endzustände auf Grund der modernen psychopharmakologischen Behandlung seltener geworden sind. Eine weitere Untersuchung widmet er der Betrachtung der Einzelsymptome und ihrer Verteilung bei verschiedenen Formen von Schizophrenie. Er registriert die Symptome nicht nur im endgültigen Zustand, sondern während des ganzen Verlaufs von Beginn der Krankheit an. Auf diese Weise kommt er zu Längsschnittbildern. Im Gefolge seiner vielseitigen Untersuchungen war es ihm möglich, Hinweise auf die Entstehung der Schizophrenien zu geben.

Ich freue mich, dass Astrup meine eigenen Forschungen aufgreifen und darauf aufbauen konnte. Noch mehr freue ich mich aber, dass er manches anders sieht, da ich mich in meinen eigenen Auffassungen dadurch bereichert fühle.

Ich bin überzeugt, dass das inhaltsreiche Buch die Anerkennung finden wird, die es verdient. Mein Wünsche begleiten es dabei.

Berlin, den 11. 11. 1977.

Prof. emerit. Dr. K. Leonhard
Bereich Medizin (Charité)
der Humboldt-Universität zu Berlin
Nervenklinik

PREFACE

The present study is based on 30 years experience with follow-ups of functional psychoses. I have come to the conclusion that what we call chronic schizophrenia is a very heterogeneous group of psychoses from a clinical point of view. The varieties of clinical symptomatology are brought fairly well into system with the Leonhard classification.

The clinical diversity of phenomenology is assosiated with marked variations of disturbed functions with psychophysiological investigations. Schizophrenia research may have been too concentrated on finding common etiological and pathophysiological factors for markedly different clinical conditions.

Comparability of findings has also been exceedingly difficult because we practically never know what types of schizophrenic patients have been studied.

The Leonhard classification system can make it possible to study the psychological and physiological pathogenetic mechanisms in homogeneous, precisely defined subgroups of schizophrenia.

ACKNOWLEDGEMENTS

I want to thank my former chiefs, professor Ørnulv Ødegård and docent Johan Bremer for all their help in carrying out the follow-up studies from Gaustad Hospital. The follow-up represents a long-term team-work, where in particular Rolf Holmboe, Arne Fossum and Kjell Noreik have made great contributions.

Financial support has been given by the Norwegian Research Council of Science and Humanities, the NIMH, Public Health Service, WHO, and the Scottish Rite Foundation. Priv. Doz. Edith Zerbin-Rüdin from the Max-Planck institute of psychiatry in Munich and professor Georg Winokur from the department of psychiatry, Iowa, have been so kind as to give valuable advice with regard to corrections of the manuscript.

CONTENTS

LIST OF TABLES

- xiii -

I. FOLLOW-UP STUDIES FROM GAUSTAD HOSPITAL

a. General background

Gaustad Hospital was opened in 1855 (Astrup & Ødegård, 1956). During the first 15 years the most frequent diagnosis was mania with 56% cured. Then followed melancholia with 37% cured. If this means complete cure, the results are scarcely better today. The patients were, however, a selection of acute and shortlasting cases with excellent prognosis.

In 1955 Holmboe (Holmboe et al., 1957) started a follow-up which gradually has been enlarged. Follow-ups have now been carried out on all first admissions to Gaustad Hospital between 1938 and 1962. In addition, clinical, social and genetic factors have been coded on admission for all patients admitted since 1963. This material is now ready for a prospective follow-up study. Retrospective follow-ups with coding principles are described in two monographs (Astrup, Fossum & Holmboe, 1962; Astrup & Noreik, 1966). The clinical series comprise about 4,500 cases.

It would probably be of interest to compare the older series with the newer ones. In particular, coding of case histories from the first 15 years might suggest to what extent symptoms have changed over the last 100 years. Preliminary reading of case histories has demonstrated that often the description of clinical symptomatology is quite as good in the old as in the modern case histories.

Evensen (1904) has followed up all male first admissions to Gaustad Hospital between 1887 and 1896 who were less than 26 years old on admission. Epileptics, imbeciles and criminals were excluded, and the follow-up period was 5 to 15 years. Among 300 admissions of functional psychoses he found 182 dementia praecox cases (61%). We had for all first admissions of functional psychoses (in 1938-50) 55 per cent with schizophrenic defects. Self-supporting schizophrenics appear to be less frequent in Evensen's series with only 15 per cent, as compared with 32 per cent in the 1938-50 series.

Evensen (1936) has also published a follow-up of 815 patients discharged from Gaustad Hospital between 1915 and 1929. In comparing these with his previous findings, Evensen points out that the social remissions of dementia praecox have increased from 15 to 23 per cent.

b. Problems of representativity

In etiological studies one would prefer to include all cases of a certain type of illness. This raises an important problem for followed-up cases from a mental hospital. They are certainly a selection of the more severe types. In a northern Norwegian community Bremer (1951) found only 13 hospitalized psychotics out of 38 cases. A follow-up with 30 years of observation period of Bremer's material is now carried out.

Preliminary results show that non-hospitalized cases predominantly are milder forms of manic-depressive and reactive psychoses. The Central Norwegian Register of psychotics was checked for all persons born in the community (Berlevåg) or living there at the time of first hospital admission since 1916.

Altogether 52 schizophrenics came from the municipality, but only 3 had never been hospitalized. This suggests that schizophrenic psychoses as a rule are hospitalized in the long run. Ødegård (1972) has calculated that the intensive population surveys do not identify more schizophrenics in the population than expected on the basis of mental hospital statistics. This implies that first admissions of schizophrenics to mental hospitals are fairly representative of schizophrenic illness in the general population.

The follow-up series from Gaustad Hospital include patients previously treated in psyciatric clinics. Comparisons with followed-up cases from the Psychiatric University Clinic in Oslo (Retterstøl, 1966 & 1970), definitely indicate that the clinic cases on the whole represent milder types of psychoses than hospitalized patients, even when given the same diagnostic labels. In any case, this must be so for the paranoid reactive psychoses where the prognosis is much better for clinic patients.

The schizophrenics may have just as good a prognosis in mental hospitals as in clinics. A large proportion of the mental hospital patients are acute violently disturbed patients who have a good prognosis, and previously were too disturbed for treatment in a clinic or at home. It should here be mentioned that drugs may have changed this aspect during recent years.

Furthermore, I would emphasize that inclusion of non-hospitalized psychoses does not necessarily give better information about the characteristics of a certain type of psychosis, as for instance, schizophrenia. My personal experience is that the vast majority of ambulatory schizophrenics I have seen, have nothing to do with Kraepelin's dementia praecox with regard to course of illness.

The borderline schizophrenics are probably genetically related to dementia praecox (Rosenthal, D. , & Kety, S.S. , 1968). Bleuler (1941) has pointed this out long ago. I would, however, prefer, like Bleuler, to give a non-psychotic diagnosis for cases without clear-cut psychotic symptoms or expected psychotic development. Considering that social psychiatric studies show 20 to 80 per cent with nervous traits in the general population, all schizophrenics will have predominantly nervous relatives. To determine what is schizophrenia-resembling nervousness must be very difficult to do, when the usual criteria of psychotic symptoms are lacking.

We also have the problem that admissions to Gaustad Hospital came from the whole country. The patients may therefore not be as representative of a definite geographical region. Noreik (1970 c) has shown, however, that the duration of illness prior to admission for 1938 through 1959 was practically the same for Gaustad as for all Norwegian mental hospitals together. This supports an assumption about representativity, duration of illness is one of the most important factors for selectivity among mental hospital admissions.

c. Comparisons between functional psychoses and other conditions

As Gaustad Hospital is a psychiatric hospital mainly for psychotic conditions, the findings are most representative for schizophrenic psychoses. The reactive and manic-depressive psychoses are predominantly the more severe types. Nevertheless, such psychoses often present differential diagnostic problems.

Followed-up patients with diagnoses of psychopathy, neuroses, alcoholic psychoses, luetic and other organic psychoses (senile and artheriosclerotic excluded) have been described (Dalgard & Noreik, 1966; Storm-Mathisen, 1969; Noreik, 1966 a; Noreik, 1966 b; Noreik, 1970 b.)

These patients are not representative of the clinical entities, as most patients with such diagnoses are treated as ambulant patients or in psychiatric clinics.

It could be ascertained that diagnoses rarely had to be changed to schizophrenia or other functional psychoses.

Yet we have not analyzed the followed-up cases with senile and artheriosclerotic psychoses. Preliminary analyses suggest the existence of a nuclear organic group with marked organic dementia and short survival period. At the other end of the spectrum are cases which, apart from being old, have a similar course of illness as manic-depression, reactive or paraphrenic cases.

Psychosis associated with mental retardation was previously diagnosed as a separate group in Norway. We have not analyzed the followed-up cases, but the findings would probably not differ much from those in a similar follow-up from Dikemark by Noreik (1972).

Epileptic psychosis has rarely been diagnosed, and represents a selection of very severe cases. Some of our cases illustrate the clinical resemblance with schizophrenia, described by Slater et al. (1965).

Up to recently very few cases with drug addiction have been treated in Gaustad Hospital. But now psychoses in connection with LSD and cannabis turn up more and more frequently.

Symptomatic psychoses may be of some interest because they often represent diagnostic alternatives to reactive psychoses. Such psychoses are, however, mainly treated in the somatic hospitals.

d. The improved prognosis in schizophrenia

From the follow-ups of Evensen (1904 and 1936) it seems that the prognosis of schizophrenia was slightly better in 1915 to 1929 as compared with 1887 to 1896.

Astrup, Fossum and Holmboe (1962) have a markedly better prognosis for 1938-50 admission. I am inclined to assume that this reflects better results with shock-treatment. But direct comparisons could not be made. By and large the prognosis appears to be the same as in Bleuler's (1972) series from the forties.

For 1951-57 admissions computer calculations gave about 10 per cent smaller risk of schizophrenic course of illness when patients had received psychotropic drugs during the first year after admission (Astrup & Noreik, 1966).

When first admission of schizophrenics 1938-50 are compared with 1958-61 admission (Holmboe, et al., 1968), the cures increased from 15 to 24 per cent. In the total series the risk of schizophrenic deterioration decreased from 43 to 24 per cent. There have not been major alterations in the diagnostic classification, but there are indications that more severe cases were treated during the last period. Thus treatment seems more effective in preventing schizophrenic deterioration than minor residuals after a functional psychotic break-down.

Like Huber (1966) we find that drug treatment has increased the tendency to development of pure ("reine") defect conditions. These are characterized by asthenia, irritability, hypochondriasis, anxiety or neuroses, or psychopathy-resembling states. Ødegård (1967) has pointed out that the flattening of affect mostly is present in such states, but not to the extent that everyday social adjustment is affected.

e. The reactive psychoses

According to the eight revision of the international classification of diseases, the functional psychoses consist of schizophrenia (295), affective psychoses (296), paranoid states (297), and other, or reactive psychoses (298).

Karl Jaspers formulated in 1913 his concept of reactive psychoses as opposed to the process psychoses. The reactive psychoses should bear relation to acute mental trauma, the psychotic content should be understandable in light of the precipitating cause, and the psychosis would tend to pass off when the cause was removed.

In the Scandinavian countries the concept of reactive or psychogenic psychoses has long traditions. The paranoid states have been included among the reactive psychoses, and in our follow-up we have made no distinction between paranoid states and acute paranoid reactions. It might perhaps be an advantage to drop this distinction because the paranoid states as a rule can be considered as reactive on the basis of personality structure and life experience.

In practice the diagnosis of reactive psychoses will often be an exclusive diagnosis when the case does not fit with the clinical diagnosis of schizophrenia or manic-depressive psychosis. We must also be aware that personality disorders and neurotic traits may be more important in the pathogenesis than mental traumas. The mental traumas are not always acute, but also contain long-standing conflicts. In addition we often observe combined psychic and somatic stress. Sometimes the differential diagnosis towards symptomatic psychoses may be difficult. Quite often alcolholic or other intoxications may be of some importance. In several cases of reactive psychoses it seems reasonable to assume that a deviating personality has manifested itself in psychic conflicts as well as in abnormal drinking.

The term reactive psychosis is mostly considered synonymous with psychogenic psychosis. But our cases are not always in accordance with Jasper's criteria. Firstly, any relation to an acute mental trauma is often absent. Secondly, the psychotic content is very often not concentrated upon a central psychic experience. Thirdly, the psychoses tend to last longer than the actual precipitating situation, and the majority of our cases have some residual symptoms. Faergeman (1963) came to similar conclusions for his followed-up reactive psychoses. For details about reactive psychoses, I will here only refer to Hirsch & Shepherd (1974).

In the United States of England cases which we call reactive psychoses are diagnosed in other groups. Some of them are included among schizophrenics and manic-depressive psychoses, others are simply not regarded as psychoses, but are to be found under neuroses, situational disturbances, etc.

Study of the literature gives us the impression that our reactive psychoses correspond to the majority of conditions called degenerative or constitutional psychoses, phasic or cycloid psychoses, abnormal reactions to experiences or schizophreniform psychoses.

The subdivision of reactive psychoses has followed several principles. One must also be aware of the fact that the clinical types are not sharply delimited from each other. Faergeman operates with emotional reactions, disorders of consciousness and paranoid types. Maniform reactions are very rare and mostly suspective of being psychoprovoked manic-depressive psychoses. Therefore, we limit the emotional group to depressive psychoses. In our follow-ups we have used the term hysterical psychosis for reactive confusion and excitation. As a rule the cases show a combination of confusion and excitation, and there is often an elated mood. Our concepts of paranoid psychosis correspond very much to Faergeman's use and includes acute paranoid reactions and more long-standing paranoid states.

In atypical cases the differential diagnosis between reactive and manic-depressive psychosis may be a problem. Roth (1960) distinguishes between endogenic and neurotic or reactive depression, and maintains that in cases of the neurotic depressive, the personality type is often unstable or psychopathic as contrary to the stable or cyclothymic personality to be found in the endogenic cases. In the neurotic reactive depression the affect is understandable as seen against the background of the patient's life history. There are no diurnal fluctuations, but the depression depends on changes in the environment. The patients are apt to have difficulties in falling asleep at night, rather than to awake early in the morning. Delusions of guilt or somatic illness are lacking in these reactive depressions, neither is there any pronounced retardation. This is in agreement with Matussek, Halbach and Troeger (1965) who use retardation, lowered vitality, and depressive feeling of guilt among the nuclear symptoms when picking out their endogenic depressive patients. It might be added that in our experience psychosomatic diseases were more frequent among reactive than endogenous psychoses (Astrup, et al., 1959 and 1963). The risk of long-term schizophrenic course of illness is comparatively small. Among 1958-61 admissions to Gaustad Hospital 9 per cent developed schizophrenic defects (Holmboe, et al., 1968).

f. The manic-depressive psychoses

The problems of differentiating endogenous and reactive depressions have already been mentioned. But for the majority of the manic-depressive psychoses, the differential diagnosis should not be difficult when the classical clinical picture is found. We have had some overlap with schizophrenia. Thus, in a series of 26 cases with mixed manic-depressive and schizophrenic symptomatology, 50 per cent developed schizophrenic defects. But among 70 cases without schizophrenic symptoms, not a single one showed a schizophrenic course of illness (Astrup, et al., 1959).

In our hospital the diagnosis of manic-depressive psychosis has been fairly reliable. Among 1938-50, 1951-57, and 1958-61 admissions 13 per cent, 0 and 5 per cent, respectively, developed schizophrenic defects. The first series comprises 117 cases, the second 38 cases, and the third 40 cases. Relapses and minor residual symptoms are as a rule found over a prolonged observation period (Holmboe, et al., 1968).

Among 175 cases with a diagnosis of manic-depressive psychosis treated in Gaustad Hospital, Noreik (1970 c) found 13 chronic cases. The concept of a chronic state means that the patients have been psychotic for the greater part of the observation period. For the circular forms, however, there will be non-psychotic phases of short duration between the melancholic and manic phases.

g. The definition of schizophrenia

If the group of schizophrenias could be distinguised more clearly from other types of functional psychoses, this would be of great advantage to determine clinical characteristics and to evaluate treatment of effects better.

When Kraepelin formulated the concept of dementia praecox in 1896 the course of illness became decisive for the diagnosis.

In the 1913 edition of his textbook, Kraepelin writes that some cases of dementia praecox may recover. He found remissions in 12.6 per cent, but those remissions did not, as a rule, last mote than three to six years. Only 2.6 per cent had lasting and stable remissions, while "social remissions" were obtained in 17 per cent. By "social remissions" Kraepelin meant that the patients somehow were able to adapt to society on their own.

When Eugen Bleuler in 1911 introduced the concept of schizophrenia, he thought that this concept corresponded to Kraepelin's dementia praecox. Bleuler did not consider it practical to base the diagnosis on the course of illness, which cannot be established until several years have passed. But in practice his concept of schizophrenia has become wider than Kraepelin's dementia praecox. This is clearly seen in the follow-ups carried out by Manfred Bleuler (1941) on schizophrenic patients classified according to the principles of Eugen Bleuler. Here, there were about equal numbers in each of the four categories of recovered, slight defects, severe defects and pronounced deterioration.

Among psychoanalytically oriented schools, there is a tendency to diagnose schizophrenia on the basis of the psychodynamic mechanisms without considering the courses of illness. In this way, the concept of schizophrenia has become broader, particularly in American psychiatry, where it includes several atypical forms, such as pseudo-neurotic schizophrenia. In a follow-up of patients with pseudo-neurotic schizophrenia, Hoch and co-workers (1962) found that only 10 per cent developed chronic schizophrenias in the long run. Thus, this conception of schizophrenia has very little in common with the Kraepelinian criteria.

Several authors maintain that it is important to distinguish between prognostically favourable and unfavourable schizophrenic psychoses. The malignant psychoses have been called genuine, nuclear, process or systematic schizophrenias. The benignant group encompasses schizo-affective states, schizophreniform psychoses, cycloid psychoses, oneirophrenia, periodic catatonia, pseudo-neurotic schizophrenia, and other atypical schizophrenic psychoses.

Langfeldt has distinguished between malignant schizophrenic process and benign schizophreniform psychoses (1937, 1939, 1960). In a 1960 paper, he claims that with careful diagnosis and follow-ups it is possible to separate these states clearly and predict correctly the long-term course of illness in 90 to 95 per cent. In his follow-ups from 1937 and 1939 Langfeldt classified his cases after the follow-up. From a methodological point of view, there is reason to be skeptical about a reclassification of patients with known outcome, especially when it fits nicely with a preconceived idea of fatal outcome in "true schizophrenia". The risk of circular reasoning is very great, and atypical traits may be more easily found in those who recover.

From my own follow-ups, and surveys of the literature, I will conclude that no sharp distinctions can be drawn between prognostically favourable and unfavourable schizophrenias in acute psychoses with schizophrenic symptomatology. A reliable prediction of schizophrenic course of illness can only be made when the schizophrenic symptoms have been present over a prolonged period, and the patients do not present affective traits or clouded consciousness.

There is a vast literature concerning the prognostic importance of individual symptoms, social and other factors. Among favourable factors can be mentioned acute onset, external precipitating factors, short duration of illness prior to hospitalization, anxiety, depression, confusion. Unfavourable factors are, for instance, a schizoid personality, low intelligence, low socio-economic level, single marital status. But none of the individual factors have decisive prognostic significance. Several authors have sought to arrive at relatively few criteria which jointly would give a maximum of information about the prognosis. By such approach it is possible to construct prognostic models which give fairly reliable prediction of the long-term course of illness.

h. Long-term outcome groups

At Gaustad Hospital all case histories have been coded in detail by two psychiatrists with regard to clinical, social and genetic factors before follow-up. Noreik and I have made independent codings for 444 cases. Our general conclusion is that psychiatric symptomatology can be coded with a fair degree of reliability. In 21 per cent of the factors coded in the whole sample there are discrepancies between the coders (Astrup & Noreik, 1966 and 1970).

In our follow-up series, long-term clinical outcome has been graded in five steps. In the worst outcome group we have those with severe schizophrenic deterioration. These comprise the subgroups of schizophrenia which Leonhard (1966) calls systematic catatonias, shallow and silly hebephrenias, confabulatory, expansive, fantastic and incoherent paraphrenia. The cases with slight schizophrenic deterioration are clear-cut schizophrenics corresponding to the classical pictures as described by Kraepelin and Bleuler. The third group is made up of patients with schizophrenic personality changes or defects, who are not so ill that they can be considered as chronic psychotics, but improved schizophrenics. These three groups we label schizophrenic outcome groups. A fourth group of improved patients includes those who show no schizophrenic personality change, but who have had psychotic relapses during the last five years, or reduced social adaption because of neurotic or psychopathic traits. Here are also included the comparatively few chronic reactive and manic-depressive psychoses. The last recovered group consists of patients who have been well for at least five years prior to re-examination.

There should not be much disagreement among psychiatrists about the patients classified by us in the groups with schizophrenic deterioration. There may be more problems in classifying patients with schizophrenic defects, partly because it is often difficult to determine whether such a defect is of a schizophrenic or neurotic type. When patients are treated with psychotropic drugs, they appear more neurotic, and an underlying schizophrenic defect may possibly be covered up.

II. LEONARD'S AND KLEIST'S CLASSIFICATION OF SCHIZOPHRENIA

a. Personal experiences

In 1955 I started a series of experimental studies of schizophrenics based on conditional reflex methods (Astrup, 1962). From preliminary studies of word associations (Astrup, 1955) I was well aware that schizophrenia is a very heterogenous group, both from a clinical and an experimental point of view. Professor Ødegård suggested that I apply the most detailed system tried out in practice, i.e. the pre-war monograph of Leonhard (1936).

In 1957 I had classified 306 chronic schizophrenics with the above mentioned system. It soon became obvious to me that the system was very difficult to apply. Therefore, I wrote to professor Leonhard, who was kind enough to send me the page proof of his new book (Leonhard, 1966). I also wrote to professor Kleist who sent me all the reprints of the classificatory work he and his pupils had carried out.

The reading was very helpful, but I still had big problems. I felt a need for discussions, and to see patients being examined and classified. This made me apply for a grant so that I could travel for 6 months, and hopefully solve some of the problems.

My first attack on the problem was to visit the hospital where Schulte von der Stein (1955) had classified patients, and ask dr. Schwab (Kleist & Schwab, 1950; Schwab, 1949) about his experiences. Very little resulted from this. Kleist, however, was very friendly, and spent many hours over several days in explaining views. In particular his demonstration of the similarities and differences between the symptoms of certain brain lesions and schizophrenia provided a logical system for bringing order into the numerous groups of symptoms. He used predominant brain mantle and brain stem symptoms, hyper- and hypoactivity as well as the possibilities of specific areas being involved, such as the frontal lobes, thalamus, striatum, caudatum, etc. (Kleist, 1957). Regardless of whether schizophrenia is an organic or a psychogenic illness, an experimental study of functions can employ the concepts of Kleist for making hypotheses about the relationships between patterns of experimental and clinical malfunctioning.

At the international congress of psychiatry in Zürich 1957 Leonhard gave a symposium on classification, and here I had the opportunity to get acquainted with the people working in this field. After the congress I spent one week with Leonhard at Charité. His assistant, dr. Baumann, spent the whole day with me. We spoke with the patients, and sometimes after, and sometimes before, Leonhard showed his examination and his arguments for placing the patient in a particular subgroup of schizophrenia. The differential diagnosis is rather complicated, because he operates with 16 typical or systematic, and three atypical or non-systematic groups of schizophrenia. What impressed me most with Leonhard was the meticulous attention he gave to details regarding the subjective experiences of the patients, and the neurological precision in the examination of the types of psychomotor disturbances. Leonhard is now retired, but is still active in research at the Charité, and I would strongly recommend those interested in classification to see the old master in action.

Kleist and Leonhard emphasized the importance of follow-ups for classification, referring to their own experiences with the Frankfurt follow-up series (Kleist, et al., 1937, 1940, 1950, 1951; Schwab, 1938, 1942, 1949; Schneider, 1955).

In 1957 we had just started a follow-up project of patients treated in Gaustad Hospital in Oslo. Kleist and Leonhard recommended that we try to validate their classificatory system in the follow-ups and we have followed their advice.

In 1957 I met Frank Fish in Zürich. He was also working with experimental and neurophysiological aspects of schizophrenia. Sir Aubrey Lewis recommended him to use the Kleist-Leonhard scheme of classification, and he classified 107 chronic female schizophrenics with a system based mainly on the definitions of Kleist (Fish, 1958 a). In the autumn of 1957 Fish and I spent a few days at St. Nicholas Hospital in Newcastle, and we saw together 103 of these cases. When the cases were reviewed, it was remarkable how often the two psychiatrists independently reached the same diagnosis, even if it was different from the author's original diagnosis. In no case was there any gross disagreement on the group to which a given case belonged. We agreed that the Leonhard system from 1957 was a marked improvement upon previous systems of classification (Fish, 1958 b).

In 1962 Fish visited Gaustad Hospital for three months, and jointly we saw

285 cases from the follow-up and the experimental series (Astrup & Fish, 1964; Fish & Astrup, 1964; Fish, 1964 a). Fish and I had now classified cases with the old master in Charité, so that we both felt safe in not mis-understanding the classificatory principles of Leonhard.

Professor Fish had a remarkable ability for systematization and synthetiza-tion as demonstrated in his monographs on schizophrenia (Fish, 1962). Also, it should be mentioned that he has provided a guide to the Leonhard classifi-cation of chronic schizophrenia in the hope that English-speaking investigators will find it useful in research projects in connection with chronic schizophrenia (Fish, 1964 b). This outline gives a logical system for classification, which is much easier to apply than the descriptions given by Leonhard.

Unfortunately, Fish died in 1967, and after his death nobody has been able to develop his ideas further. I shall now make an attempt at continuing the work of Fish with systematization of the evaluation of the Kleist-Leonhard schemes.

b. The history of the Kleist-Leonhard classification

While Kraepelin and Bleuler created the concept of schizophrenia, it is often forgotten that there are other traditions in European psychiatry. Thus the French psychiatrists at the end of the last century described a variety of types of psychoses in great detail (Ey, 1958). Russian psychiatry is heavily in-fluences by French psychiatry, and a major research project reflects this with regard to the clinical classification of schizophrenia (Snezhnevsky, 1972). Kraepelin himself gave many descriptions of schizophrenic subgroups, but put less emphasis on distinguising subgroups than demonstrating the common ele-ments of the illness.

Wernicke (1906) is a representative of the neurophysiological orientation of Griesinger, and as an eminent neurologist he studied the psychiatric clinical symptoms in meticulous detail, pointed for instance out the existence of the prognostically favourable cycloid psychoses. Kleist was a pupil of Wernicke, and was brought up in this tradition, with attempts at differentiating the clinical symptoms as much as possible. As pointed out by Janzarik (1969), their noso-graphic points of view can be considered the antithesis of the unitary psychosis. But according to Hegelian dialectics, thesis and antithesis are necessary for synthesis, which in psychiatric classifications means the understanding of the often arbitrary classes among phenomena with complex common, as well as different elements.

Kleist and Leonhard assume that organic and genetic factors play a dominant
role in the etiology of schizophrenia. The Kleistian theories of cerebral locali-
zation seem to be difficult to accept today. Leonhard thinks that his 19 subgroups are due to specific genetic factors. Furthermore, he operates with
combined forms in analogy to certain genetically determined neurological disorders. For the 16 subgroups of systematic schizophrenia, this gives theoret-
ically 120 combinations. From a practical point of view such a complicated
system can scarcely be used. Fish and I think that each subgroups represents
only a typical symptom constellation. There are all kinds of intermediate
symptoms, and we chose to classify the patients in the subgroups which they
resemble the most, according to the decision rules specified by Fish (1964 b).
In discussion with Leonhard in 1966, he had no objection to these principles
of classification, although he believed that the use of combinatory forms might
be more adequate for the understanding of deficits of functioning.

Many believe that the Kleistians disregard psychological factors, which is
an unjustified criticism. Kleist told me about his milieu treatment of chronic
shhizophrenics, where one element was to let patients dine with him and his
family. I think most modern psychotherapists would not be as accepting as
letting the chronic schizophrenics live with their own families. The skepticism
toward theories of a psychodynamic etiology of schizophrenia has, on the other
side, led to added emphasis on psychological treatment of conditions where
psychodynamic factors are probably of central importance. Thus both Kleist
and Leonhard have differentiated typical psychogenic psychoses from the endogenous psychosis. Leonhard has also developed an individual psychotherapy
of neuroses, which represents a kind of behaviour therapy long before the term
behaviour therapy was invented (Leonhard, 1965). Leonhard (1969) pointed out
the inadvisability of labeling as schizophrenics the cycloid psychoses which
can be predicted to recover regardless of whether they receive any somatic
or psychological treatment.

Henri Ey (1959) has tried out the Leonhard-Kleist classifications. At the
time this work was done, all literature was written in German, and Henri Ey
does not speak German. It is very impressive that he, nevertheless, could use
the scheme. The reason for this is obviously that practically all the Kleist-
Leonhard subgroups are described under other names in the French psychiatric literature.

Sarro Burbano and co-workers (Sarro et al. , 1950; Coderch, et al. , 1957) have studied Spanish chronic schizophrenics. Sarro Burbano represents the existentialistic psychiatric school, and thinks that the German and Spanish schizophrenias differ, but finds the system useful. He points out that the fantastic subgroup is characterized by absurd ideas in German patients, while the Spanish patients have a relatively coherent antropocosmological and magic structure. His analysis represents an improvement upon the descriptions by Leonhard from 1936, showing that a series of specific existentialistic experiences tend to go together. I have found the same symptoms in Norwegian patients (Astrup, 1962). But I am skeptical about the chronic schizophrenics being essentially different in the various cultures. I have studied in some detail German, English, American and Russian patients, and the Leonhard subgroups show the same characteristics in all of those populations. It is harder to judge from the literature from other countries, because many of the characteristic symptoms are not elicited unless the examiner knows what to look for.

Janzarik (1961) followed 100 schizophrenics over practically the whole course of life through the case histories. He had a few cases who for decades remained catatonic from the beginning. But the vast majority of the psychoses went through a paranoid hallucinatory stage. He emphasized also that change of symptoms is more characteristic than constancy.

In my opinion Janzarik is right concerning the changing symptoms during initial stages. Over prolonged periods things are more complicated. In a series of 990 followed-up patients with schizophrenic defects only 14% had no delusions, and 15% no hallucinations during the acute stage (Astrup, 1969). This supports the assumption that most schizophrenics have a paranoid-hallucinatory period. Very often schizophrenic psychoses show combinations of syndromes. Thus, initially 29% had hebephrenic and 19% catatonic syndromes. The final outcome was estimated as paranoid for 59%, catatonic for 17%, and hebephrenic for 24%. When the syndromes are combined, the catatonic and hebephrenic syndromes tend to be more decisive than the paranoid syndromes for the final outcome.

Marked fluctuations and changes in symptoms over many years are especially characteristic of the atypical or non-systematic schizophrenias, which made up 45%. As a rule the systematic schizophrenias change very much over the first 5 to 10 years. But when the stable defect condition is established, the same type tends to be found over many years, at least for personal re-examinations after 16-17 years (Flekkøy & Astrup, 1975). Here the reservation is taken that the expansive-fantastic ideas often develop after more than 10 years duration of illness. Furthermore, drugs seem to influence the final stages. However, this will be discussed in more detail later in this book.

The Kleist-Leonhard classifications have undergone many changes over the years. Initially Kleist defined the types on the basis of very few observations. The original material of Leonhard (1936) was of a considerable size, but comprised only chronic inmates of the Gabersee mental hospital. The later follow-ups and accumulation of new cases by Leonhard (1966) showed comparatively more of the benign non-systematic types, which now could be defined more precisely. As late as in 1961 (Leonhard, 1961) the non-systematic paranoid type is renamed from schizophasia to cataphasia to illustrate the admixture of psychomotor symptoms and thought disturbances. In fact, the three non-systematic types of periodic catatonia, schizophasia (cataphasia) and affect-laden paraphrenia are very often difficult to distinguish from each other, particularly in the initial stages.

I have not been convinced about the advisability of redefining schizophasia to cataphasia. Leonhard thinks that the non-systematic schizophrenias are the malignant relatives ("bösartige Verwandten") of the cycloid psychoses. The periodic catatonias are the relatives of the motility psychoses, affect-laden paraphrenia the relative of anxiety- ecstasy psychoses, and schizophasia the relatives of stupor-confusion psychoses. As the latter show both speech disorder and psychomotor disturbances, Leonhard thought that the schizophasias should also be characterized by combinations of speech and psychomotor disorders of non-catatonic type and renamed cataphasia. I feel this distinction to be too subtle and include all non-systematic cases with predominant psychomotor disturbances in the group of periodic catatonia.

Leonhard includes cases with expansive ideas among the affect-laden paraphrenias, maintaining that even with severely deteriorated cases he can distinguish between the severely blunted systematic cases and those with maintained elements of affective responses. I include only the paranoia-resembling expansive cases. This seems justified in view of the changes which occurred with systematic expansive cases which in the drug era have much more affective responsiveness than previously. If they should be included among the non-systematic affect-laden paraphrenias, this would highly disturb comparability with pre-drug series.

Russian investigators make a distinction between shift-life and steady developing subgroups of schizophrenia, which in principle corresponds very much to the distinction between systematic and non-systematic schizophrenia (Snezhnevsky, 1972).

Japanese investigators have, like Leonhard, maintained that the atypical psychoses should rather be considered as independent intermediate species between schizophrenic and manic-depressive psychoses, than admixtures of the two types, because of mixed genetic background, such as advocated from the Tübingen school (Mitsuda, 1967, p. 74).

Basit (1972) compared 20 systematic and 20 non-systematic schizophrenias who were clinically diagnosed by Fish. Fish hypothesized that the former should be characterized by retardation, and the latter by thought disorder. Basit could not confirm this hypothesis and concluded that he could not provide evidence that there is any significant difference between the two major groups as proposed by Leonhard. However, Basit mentions in the discussion that Leonhard did not maintain that the difference is based on such criteria. My own prolonged experience with testing of schizophrenic patients (Astrup, 1962; Flekkøy & Astrup, 1975) makes me skeptical about the possibility that the tests used by Basit should differentiate between the two types of psychosis. A number of subjects had to be excluded because they were unable to co-operate sufficiently. My guess is that these were predominantly of the systematic types which very often are not testable at all with psychological test procedures, such as reproduction of responses in the word association test (Flekkøy & Astrup, 1975).

At the present state of knowledge, the Leonhard system should only be considered as a scheme of classification applied without any preconceived ideas about physiological or somatic etiology. I have suggested that the development of the schizophrenic process can be understood in reflexological terms, but the classification system can just as well be used by adherents of psychodynamic pathogenesis. Fish has proposed an interesting neuro-physiological model of the differences between systematic and non-systematic schizophrenia, but I do not think any of the experimental studies, including my own, have shown specific differences. The main difference is that the systematic schizophrenias perform works on practically all tests in unbiased samples. This only shows that the clinically worse patients perform less well.

c. Decision rules for separating the Leonhard subgroups of chronic schizophrenia

I prefer to start by establishing whether the patient has delusions or hallucinations. If expansive delusions are present the patient will be classified as a severely deteriorated paranoid unless he has the extremely rare paranoia-resembling type of affect-laden paraphrenia. The four types of severe deterioration are expansive, confabulatory, fantastic and incoherent paraphrenia. There appear to be gradual transitions between the two first comparatively monosymptomatic types to the fantastic cases with no limits between death and life, and all-embracing fantastic experiences, to the incoherent who are too sick to express such complex ideas as the fantastic cases (Astrup, et al., 1962). The next step is to see whether the patient has a chronic hallucinatory psychosis, which is classified as mild systematic defect. Here the phonemic paraphrenia is characterized by auditory hallucinations, while the hypocondriacal paraphrenia has auditory as well as haptic hallucinations. The remaining paranoid cases are mild defects of non-systematic type. If affectively charged delusions dominate or have dominated the clinical picture, the subgroup is affect-laden paraphrenia. These psychoses respond very well to drugs, so that now the delusions only flare up periodically. When speach disturbances dominate, the subtype is schizophasia. Here also the drugs have marked effects. Neologisms and word salad are rarely seen. I usually give a few proverbs to interpret in order to elicit the typical speech and thought disturbances. These patients are well ordered in behaviour even if the speech disturbances are marked.

The next step is to sort out the catatonic schizophrenias. The milder defects with some akinesias or periodic hyperkinesias belong to the non-systematic periodic catatonia group. When the patient is able to communicate verbally, the "Vorbeireden" or talking beside the point is very characteristic of speech-prompt catatonia. The parakinetic catatonia is usually recognized by the jerking movements which resemble choreiform movements. The proskinetic catatonia shows "Mitgehen", that is, the patient allows his body to be moved by the slightest pressure made by the examiner. For manneristic catatonia the most characteristic feature is "Gegenhalten", or opposition. Any attempt by the examiner to move the patient's body leads to an almost equivalent increase of tension in the opposing muscles, so that it is difficult for the examiner to move the patient's body. Negativistic catatonia is characterized by a true negativism, that is an active striving against all attempts to make contact with the patient. The last group of systematic catatonia is the speech-inactive form. When spoken to, these patients give no answers, but can be seen to be whispering, and appear to be completely preoccupied by auditory hallucinations. For details concerning the differential diagnosis of systematic catatonias, the guide of classification by Fish (1964) is very helpful.

All hebephrenic types of schizophrenia are considered systematic. Usually they have an insidious onset, while the non-systematic schizophrenias tend to have an acute onset of illness. Here I also make a distinction between mild and severe defects. The severe defects tend to have a euphoric mood, and in any case a marked flattening of affect. The silly or "läppische" hebephrenics are well known from the descriptions of Kraepelin, and are easily recognized. A smiling, or a pronounced giggling, is particularly characteristic, and this becomes prominent under the influence of every external stimulus. Usually, the shallow hebephrenics are able to carry on a simple conversation, but give no emotional response when topics which should affect them are discussed. The mood is usually cheerful or contented, but periodically the patients may be hallucinated, irritable, aggressive and excited.

The mild hebephrenic defects have affective changes in the direction of irritability, dysphoria, discontent and cheerlessness. The autistic hebephrenics actively shut themselves up, avoid all contacts with others, and tend to reject attempts from others to associate with them. They resemble very much paranoid schizophrenics, and were originally classified as paranoid cases by Leonhard (1936). Later he considered the classification within the hebephrenic group as most adequate because of the affective flattening. The eccentric hebephrenics have an affective flattening as the central symptomatology. They may also give the impression of being depressed, and often have hypochondrical complaints. The patients are stereotyped in their verbal utterances, and often show eccentric and manneristic behaviour. Many patients collect worthless things, may carry out compulsive movements, have rituals of praying, eat only special kinds of food, etc.

For many purposes it is not practical to operate with all 19 subgroups. Besides the distinction between systematic and non-systematic cases, the distinctions between paranoid, catatonic and hebephrenic cases, or the distinctions between severe and mild defects may be most appropriate for the clinical problem studied. It should also be mentioned that many of the non-systematic and mild hebephrenic defects represent more personality deviations than chronic psychotic states. Among the 990 cases referred to previously, there were 135 paranoid, 48 catatonic and 66 hebephrenic cases who had no overt psychotic symptoms.

For the classification of patients into major subgroups, such as systematic and non-systematic schizophrenias, a good case history is usually sufficient.

For classification into the 19 subgroups a personal examination is preferable, especially for the systematic catatonias where the types of motor disturbances have to be elicited with special techniques. For the other subgroups, the characteristic features are so often mentioned in the case histories, that I usually only confirm the classification from case history during the personal examination.

d. Genetic aspects

Among the 530 patients in the original material of Leonhard (1936) 440 were typical and 90 atypical cases. Only 5 per cent of the former and 37 per cent of the latter had relatives hospitalized for endogenous psychoses.

Schulz and Leonhard (1940) made a study of the genetic background of typical and atypical schizophrenia. The case material had been genetically studied by Schulz and hospitalized cases in the neighbourhood of Munich were classified by Leonhard, who had no information about the genetic findings. In this study the atypical cases had only slightly more schizophrenic relatives than the typical cases, with, for instance, 7.8 and 5.6 per cent siblings, and 5.5 and 9 per cent parents, respectively, with schizophrenic psychoses. I visited Munich in 1957, and Schulz was kind enough to let me read the case histories of the 54 typical and 45 atypical cases as well as giving me the genetic information. My impression was that this methodically correct comparison of genetic background in the two types came so early that Leonhard had not properly elaborated the clinical differential diagnosis. New comparative studies should probably be carried out, using the same methods as Schulz and Leonhard. It is possible that the genetic differences will turn out as promising as for Leonhard's bi-polar and uni-polar affective psychoses (Perris, 1966).

For a series of 1678 followed-up consecutive admissions of functional psychoses to Gaustad Hospital, we have compared the clinical types with the types of psychoses in the case history of 824 relatives. There were case histories of 35 grandparents, 159 parents, 222 uncles and aunts, and 408 siblings (Astrup, et al. , 1962 and 1966). The genetic background of the Leonhard subgroups is shown in Table I (887 with schizophrenic defects).

The non-systematic schizophrenias have 36 per cent of the psychotic relatives with identical clinical pictures as compared with 14 per cent for the systematic cases. Non-systematic schizophrenias had 52% relatives with the same types of schizophrenias while systematic schizophrenias had 48%. Both

Table 1. First admissions with schizophrenic defects 1938-1957

Types of probands	Psychotic relatives with available case histories	Of whom with identical pictures	No. of suicides	No. of probands
Affect-laden paraphrenia	109	40	13	210
Schizophasia	56	17	7	89
Phonemic paraphrenia	30	6	2	85
Hypochondriacal paraphrenia	24	6	1	56
Confabulatory paraphrenia	2	0	0	11
Expansive paraphrenia	10	0	0	21
Fantastic paraphrenia	16	5	1	36
Incoherent paraphrenia	8	1	1	11
Autistic hebephrenia	13	0	2	34
Eccentric hebephrenia	40	3	7	90
Shallow hebephrenia	36	3	4	54
Silly hebephrenia	8	0	6	27
Periodic catatonia	96	37	1	90
Parakinetic catatonia	7	1	0	11
Speech-prompt catatonia	3	2	0	10
Proskinetic catatonia	3	2	0	7
Speech-inactive catatonia	4	0	2	20
Manneristic catatonia	11	0	2	14
Negativistic catatonia	1	1	1	11
Total	477	124	50	887

groups had 28 per cent with reactive and manic-depressive psychoses which might contradict the assumption that the atypical cases are mixed schizo-phrenic-affective from a genetic point of view, as maintained by the Tübingen school. (Table 2). The non-systematic schizophrenias have markedly more psychotic siblings than the systemic cases. (Table 3.)

Table 2. Distribution of psychoses among relatives of patients with systematic and non-systematic schizophrenia.

Probands	Type of psychoses among relatives				
	systematic schiz.	non-syste-matic schiz.	reactive	manic-depres-sive	total
Systematic schizophrenia	48%	24%	15%	13%	100%
Non-systematic schizophrenia	20%	52%	13%	15%	100%

Table 3. Hospitalized functional psychoses among siblings of followed-up psychoses.

Types of followed-up psychoses	No. of siblings with functional psychoses		Hospitalized psychotic siblings per 100 cases
	Sisters	Brothers	
Non-systematic schizophrenia	75	78	39,4
Systematic schizophrenia	63	64	25,5

We have 1.56 times more cases histories of relatives of non-systematic than of systematic schizophrenias. The same tendency holds true for probably psychotic relatives without available case histories. This suggests that the total genetic loading of psychoses is larger for the non-systematic than for the systematic schizophrenias, as assumed by Leonhard (1936, 1966).

For the total material Ødegård (1972) has calculated the genetic loading and suggested from these data that the hereditary factors in functional psychoses probably are polygenetic. In table 2 the genetic background of each type of relative is listed for systematic and non-systematic schizophrenia.

Table 2 shows that the relatives of both types of psychoses have a strong tendency to present similar types of psychoses. Many Japanese investigators have pointed out that the probands with atypical psychoses predominantly have relatives with such psychoses as well (Mitsuda, 1967). Russian investigators find much more genetic tainting in atypical than in typical schizophrenia (Snezhnevsky, 1972). Thus, data from many countries suggest that the genetic heterogeneity of schizophrenia may be reduced by separate studies of systematic and non-systematic types.

From the published case histories of concordant monocyotic twins of Kringlen (1967), Fischer (1973), and Slater (1953), I classified all cases with detailed information about the clinical pictures into systematic and non-systematic schizophrenia, as well as non-schizophrenic psychoses. The latter category was used for cases with schizophrenic symptoms, which did not develop defect states. In comparison with these data I classified the discordant monocyotic twins of Kringlen (1964, 1967), Fischer (1973), Tienari (1963), and Slater (1953) in the same clinical categories. The results are shown in tables 4 and 5.

Table 4 shows that the concordant twins are predominantly of the non-systematic type. The discordant twins are predominantly systematic schizophrenics. Table 1 showed that non-systematic schizophrenia had more genetic homogeneity than systematic schizophrenia. External factors also have a greater tendency to precipitate the non-systematic, than the systematic schizophrenias (Astrup, et al., 1962). Thus, the non-systematic schizophrenias are the most

Table 4. Differentiation of concordant monocygotic twins according to subtype of schizophrenia.

Both twins	nonsystematic schizophrenia	44
"	" systematic schizophrenia	24
"	" nonschizophrenic psychosis	16
"	" different subgroups	8

Table 5. Discordant monozygotic twins

Clinical groups	Kringlen	Fischer	Tienari	Slater	Total
Systematic schizophrenia	13	7	13	9	42
Non-systematic schizophrenia	10	1	1	4	16
Non-schizophrenic psychosis	1	0	3	0	4
Not classifiable	1	3	0	0	4
Total	25	11	17	13	66

genetically, as well as the most environmentally, determined psychoses. The lack of concordance in the series of Tienari might be explained by most of his cases being systematic. The probable reason for this is that the psychoses in his series started early in life compared with other series.

The comparison of clinical pictures in monozygotic twins can, of course, only give valid results if performed without knowledge of the presence or absence of illness in the co-twin. I hope to be able to do such a controlled study later.

e. The relative frequencies of systematic and non-systematic schizophrenias

In the original material of Leonhard (1936) the atypical cases made up 17 per cent. In my own series of 306 chronic schizophrenias classified 1955-57 (Astrup, 1962) there were 19 per cent atypical cases, while first admissions 1938-60 with schizophrenic outcome were 45 per cent. Thus, the non-systematic cases are much more frequent among consecutive first admissions. This reflects that the chronic hospital population is composed of the more severely deteriorated systematic cases which accumulate over many years. In the municipality of Berlevåg (pop. 1800) there are currently 15 persons with schizophrenic and schizophreniform psychoses. All but 3 have previous hospitalizations. I have personally examined those 15 cases. Only one patient had a systematic schizophrenia, and that of the mild paranoid type. Nine were non-systematic and five schizophreniform. This illustrates that comparatively few systematic schizophrenics are able to live independent lives in the community.

f. Changes over prolonged time periods

Fish and I (1964) re-classified jointly 285 chronic schizophrenics in 1962 at Gaustad Hospital. Changes in the clinical pictures of chronic schizophrenics classified four years previously were very uncommon. 14% of the patients were reclassified, but in only 5% did the reclassification involve a transfer between the slight and severe defect groups as defined in part c. of this chapter. In cases where the previous classification had been made by personal examination, the diagnostic error was 9%, whereas in cases classified on the basis of the case histories the error was 31%. As the Leonhard scheme consists of 19 subgroups, the diagnostic error in the personally classified cases is surprisingly small.

In 1972 I reclassified 148 patients after a mean observation period of 10 years. This time there was also a fair constancy of the clinical classification as seen from table 6.

Now there is a tendency to improvement over the years. I suspect that the changes are real, and not merely errors in classification. They may reflect the tendency to improvement with increasing age, emphasized by Bleuler (1972). But I also think the drugs have contributed to the transitions from more severe to milder defect stages.

A series of 219 functional psychoses was followed up in 1956, and re-examined in 1966 (Noreik, et al., 1967). In this material 134 patients were classified as chronic schizophrenics in 1956. Their 1966 classification is shown in table 7.

Table 7 shows that 39 patients have moved from schizophrenic to non-schizophrenic outcome. These were originally, as a rule, not considered to be psychotic, but had schizophrenic personality deviations. Only six of the originally non-schizophrenic cases were in 1966 considered to be schizophrenics. Thus, there is a tendency for the schizophrenic symptoms to fade away over the years. The table also shows that there is a relative decrease of the severe stages.

Table 6. Clinical classification at first follow-up and at re-examination 1972

Classification at re-examination 1972	Classification at first follow-up								
	Non-systematic mild paranoid	Non-systematic mild catatonic	Systematic mild paranoid	Systematic mild hebephrenic	Systematic severe paranoid	Systematic severe hebephrenic	Systematic severe catatonic	Non-schizophrenic functional psychoses	TOTAL
Non-systematic mild paranoid	30	2	2		3		1	1	39
Non-systematic mild catatonic		13					6		19
Systematic mild paranoid	3		13			2			18
Systematic mild hebephrenic	1			13		4	0	1	19
Systematic severe paranoid	6	2	4	1	13	3	1	1	31
Systematic severe hebephrenic				1		12			13
Systematic severe catatonic							9		9
Non-schizophrenic functional psychoses								10	10
TOTAL	40	17	19	15	16	21	17	13	158

Table 7

1966 Classification

1956 Classification	Affect-laden paraphrenia	Schizophasia	Phonemic paraphrenia	Hypocondrial paraphrenia	Confabulatory paraphrenia	Expansive paraphrenia	Fantastic paraphrenia	Inkoherent paraphrenia	Autistic hebephrenia	Eccentric hebephrenia	Shallow hebephrenia	Silly hebephrenia	Periodic catatonia	Parakinetic catatonia	Speech-prompt catatonia	Proskinetic catatonia	Speech-inactive catatonia	Manneristic catatonia	Negativistic catatonia	Non-schizo-phrenic	Total
Affect-laden paraphrenia	9	3	1	1																15	29
Schizophasia		3											1							3	7
Phonemic paraphrenia	2	1	5	1		1				1										2	13
Hypochondrial paraphrenia		1		5	1					1										1	9
Confabulatory paraphrenia					1																1
Expansive paraphrenia		1				2	1														4
Fantastic paraphrenia	1						5											1		1	8
Incoherent paraphrenia				1		1											1				3
Autistic hebephrenia		2							2	2										2	8
Eccentric hebephrenia										3	1									5	9
Shallow hebephrenia										1	1	1	1								4
Silly hebephrenia											1	2	1								4
Periodic catatonia	1	3								1			12							10	27
Parakinetic catatonia																					0
Speech-prompt catatonia															1	1					2
Proskinetic catatonia																					0
Speech-inactive catatonia		1				1							3								5
Manneristic catatonia																					0
Negativistic catatonia													1								1
Non-schizophrenic																					
Total	13	14	7	8	2	5	6	0	2	9	3	3	20	0	1	1	1	0	0	39	134

Among 95 patients with schizophrenic outcome in both follow-ups 51 were classified in identical Leonhard subgroups. This is a fair agreement. With 19 subgroups the 46 per cent discrepancies represent only 2 per cent of all coding alternative by pure chance.

Among 63 cases classified as non-systematic in 1956, 32 were non-systematic in 1966, 28 had non-schizophrenic outcome, while 3 were considered to be systematic cases.

This shows that the non-systematic schizophrenias with their tendency to periodic exacerbations account for most of the shifts to non-schizophrenic outcome. It is also noted, with three exceptions, that those with schizophrenic defects remained within the similar categories of non-systematic schizophrenia.

Also for cases of systematic schizophrenia most discrepancies in classification are accounted for by similar subgroups. Among paranoid systematic defects, 30 or 34 remain in the paranoid categories. Fourteen of 18 hebephrenics remain hebephrenic, and six of eight systematic catatonias remain catatonic. Our findings thus contradict those of Janzarik (1961) about marked shifts in types of schizophrenic defects over long observation periods.

In comparing followed-up admissions to Gaustad Hospital from 1938-50 and 1951-60, it turned out that the percentages of severe paranoid defects decreased from 19 to 11 per cent of all paranoid defects. For catatonic psychoses the severe systematic defects showed between 1930-57 and 1958-60 a decrease from 45 to 24 per cent. The severe hebephrenic defects made up 9 per cent of all 1938-57 admissions and 2 per cent of all 1958-60 admissions. This shows that all types of severe deteriorations have become less frequent during the later periods. The systematic catatonias seem to disappear, because the last such case among chronic hospital cases in 1972 was admitted as early as 1952. (Flekkøy & Astrup, 1975.)

I think that adequate drug treatment from the first admission largely prevents the development of severe systematic defects.

g. Effects of drug treatment

As early as in 1958 I had an impression that the non-systematic schizophrenias benefited more from psychotropic drugs than the systematic schizophrenias (Astrup, 1959 & 1962). This impression has been confirmed in a double-blind study of neuroleptics, where the classification was made independent of the evaluation of the clinical effects of treatment (Astrup, et al., 1974).

Fish and I tried to evaluate the effects of different types of drug on 474 chronic schizophrenics (Astrup & Fish, 1964). No drugs seemed to have specific effects on any of the 19 Leonhard subgroups, but the sample of treated patients was too small to get valid conclusions. On the whole, the newer drugs did not appear to have better effects than chlorpromazine. Most improvement was seen in the non-systematic cases. Fish (1964 a) found that the phonemic and hypochondriacal paraphrenia, eccentric and autistic hebephrenias responded better than other systematic schizophrenias, which means more effect in mild than severe defects. The response in the systematic catatonics was in particular poor, but over very prolonged observation periods (15-17 years) even a few of the systematic catatonias appear to improve (Flekkøy & Astrup, 1975).

Part f of this chapter suggests that the drugs to a great extent can prevent severe schizophrenic deterioration. We have previously calculated with multivariate techniques that drugs reduce the long-term risk of schizophrenic defects with about 10 per cent, as compared with the shock treatments (Astrup & Noreik, 1966). This seems to imply that the schizo-affective psychoses especially have a much better prognosis. Instead of developing a non-systematic schizophrenia, a considerable proportion recover and can, with respect to long-term prognosis, be classified as cycloid psychoses.

An important consequence of this is that the relationship between course of illness in probands and their relatives will change with time. If, for instance, the probands are treated in the drug era and most of their relatives before that time, the relatives will tend to have more severe types of defects. Comparing the distribution of the Leonhard subgroups in four series consisting of 1938-50 and 1951-57 series and their relatives, this factor led, however, only to minor alterations. The reason for this is probably that only a small proportion of the probands in the last series and the relatives were treated with drugs at the initial stage of the illness (Astrup & Noreik, 1966).

As pointed out by Ødegård (1967), the schizophrenics have changed very much since the days of Kraepelin. Huber (1966) finds in follow-ups a great percentage of undercharacteristic residual states, which are called "reine Defektsyndrome". We have similar findings. When 1938-50 admissions are compared with 1958-61 admissions, the clinical outcome in the latter series is characterized by much fewer cases with overt psychotic symptoms and more with schizophrenic personality changes. The latter are classified as belonging to the non-systematic and mild hebephrenic defects. They are often difficult to distinguish from residual states after manic-depressive and reactive psychoses, especially when under prolonged treatment with neuroleptic drugs (Holmboe, et al., 1968).

h. Psychosocial treatment

I think it has been established that symptomatically, the schizophrenias have a considerably milder course of illness in the drug era than before. Some optimists have predicted that this soon will empty the mental hospitals. The Camberwell register (Wing & Hailey, 1972) shows a clear-cut reduction of old long-stay patients, but this is almost balanced by a build-up of new types of long-stay patients.

I have previously mentioned the improved prognosis found by re-examination in 1966, and in patients followed-up for the first time in 1956. The symptomatological improvement was not associated with a better working ability or other signs of better social adjustment. The percentage of patients treated in mental hospital was practically the same at the two follow-ups.

Comparing 1938-50, 1951-57 and 1958-61 admissions, the marked clinical improvement over those years is not associated with better working capacity at follow-up. There may be social factors accounting for this. One obvious difference is that before 1961 patients with handicaps discharged from hospitals either had to work or were boarded out on farms. After 1961 persons with mental handicaps are entitled to invalid pensions.

But certain important questions can be raised. The first is whether the symptomatological improvement is associated with side effects so that the net gain in social adaption is small. The second question is whether psychological and social treatments have been inadequate for attaining better adjustment. The 19 subgroups of chronic schizophrenia with the marked variations within some subgroups, such as the non-systematic types, demonstrate clearly the heterogeneity of schizophrenia. It may be questioned whether present psychological and social treatments are sufficiently differentiated to meet the needs of the very different types of patients.

i. Neurophysiological aspects

The chronic schizophrenics can be regarded as an experiment of nature, where certain rather specific systems have changed functions over prolonged periods. Increased knowledge about the psycho-physiology of schizophrenia might not only teach us more about schizophrenia, but also about basic brain mechanisms.

In principle I would consider the Leonhard subgroups as a useful classification for neurophysiological research, as it is probably easier to find characteristic deficits of function in clinically well defined and homogenous groups than in the whole heterogenous group of schizophrenias. A far-fetched analogy would be that Følling's disease could not have been discovered among oligophrenics with the "schizophrenic research strategy" of, for instance, getting mean biochemical values of urines from 1000 patients.

My own attempts at comparing the Leonhard subgroups with conditional reflex techniques have failed so far in that no specific differences could be found
(Astrup, 1962). But I was able to demonstrate vast differences between the
subgroups with respect to general impairment of functions as measured by
word associations, motor conditional reflexes, unconditional defensive reflexes
and various types of autonomic measures.

It is outside the scope of this paper to discuss the neurophysiology of schizophrenia in detail. I would only mention that there are such variations over time
in clinical conditions and experimental findings that the illness can hardly be
of an organic type corresponding to general paresis or the organic dementias.
It is also unlikely that the pathogenesis corresponds to the psychodynamic
developments in neurotic disorders. In the latter, the functional disturbances
are centered around psychological complex structures, as measured with strong
autonomic responses to complex words, although some minor general disturbances of functions can be found. In the schizophrenics general disturbances
prevail, often of a magnitude just as pronounced as in organic psychoses, in
particular in the systematic catatonias. The affect-laden paraphrenias resemble the neurosis and psychogenic psychoses insofar as there are strong
autonomic responses to complex words. But prolonged studies of cases suggest that the initial stage is often characterized by general disturbances, clinically as well as experimentally. The affect-laden delusions need some time
to develop, and it seems to be the same case for the strong autonomic responses
to stimulus words related to the delusions. It is possible that schizophrenia is
a conglomerate of illnesses on the scale from purely organic to purely psychogenic conditions. My personal hypothesis is, however, that the group of schizophrenias are genetically determined general reaction types to the most varied
forms of stress. I think also that the pathogenetic mechanisms may be explained in the terms of Gantt's concepts of autokinesis and schizokinesis which
were established experimentally. These disturbances are in principle revers-
ible, but may proceed apparently without relation to external stress when first
initiated. Whether biochemical changes are primary or secondary to the reaction types will be up to future research to find out.

III. GENERAL CHARACTERISTICS OF A MATERIAL OF CHRONIC SCHIZOPHRENICS

The present material is composed of all first admissions to Gaustad Hospital during the years 1938-60 who developed schizophrenic defects later. The patients have been followed up during the years 1955 to 1972. The minimum observation period is 5 years, which normally is sufficient to establish the long-term courses of illness. Some patients have very long observation periods since first admission, up to 34 years. The total material comprises 990 patients.

Through the population registers and other sources we were able to locate all patients living in Norway, but some having emigrated to other countries could not be found. It might be mentioned that the Scandinavian countries offer good opportunities for long-term follow-ups because the population is well registered. There is also markedly less mobility than in the larger countries, such as the USA and the USSR. Furthermore, Norway is a sparsely populated country, where people know much about each other, so that the few who had escaped official registration also could be traced.

As far as practically possible, discharged patients were seen in their homes by a team of psychiatrists. For financial reasons we had to limit the personal follow-up to eastern and south-eastern Norway, within a distance of 400 kilometers from the hospital. The team of doctors have driven altogether about 300 000 kilometers by car to carry out the follow-up.

For patients living outside the geographically limited area, information was obtained from public health officers (mainly patients under psychiatric care), relatives and questionnaires to the patients. All patients residing in Gaustad Hospital at the time of re-examination were seen personally. For patients treated in other hospitals we found it more practical to base our evaluation on the case histories and the reports of our colleagues about the course of illness.

Clinical symptomatology at admission, social and genetic background were

coded in great detail as described by Astrup & Noreik (1966). All coding was
carried out before the follow-up started, in order to avoid, as much as possible, that the coding should be biased by knowledge about the outcome of the
illness.

In the group of atypical paranoid schizophrenia there were 230 cases with
affect-laden paraphrenia, and 119 cases with schizophasia. Altogether 251
patients were personally re-examined in their homes or at Gaustad Hospital.
For 90 cases information was obtained from other hospitals, public health
officers or relatives. Eight persons outside the area with personal follow-
up answered questionnaires, and additional information was provided from
other sources. In the atypical paranoid schizophrenias the defects are milder
that in typical schizophrenias, and 88 of the affect-laden, and 47 of the schizophasic cases had only schizophrenic personality change without overt psychotic
symptoms.

In the initial stages the atypical paranoid schizophrenias are often rather
similar, and even in the chronic stages they may show admixtures or symptoms of other groups. They often present schizo-affective symptomatology at
the onset with a strong tendency to remissions and periodic course of illness.
Many cases correspond to the paranoias and systematic paraphrenias of
Kraepelin (1910), or the paranoid psychoses with systematized delusions of
French authors (Ey, 1959). There will often be doubt as to whether these
psychoses should be classified as schizophrenias.

In a group of chronic hallucinatory schizophrenics there were 90 cases with
phonemic and 61 cases with hypochondriacal schizophrenia. 102 cases were
personally interviewed at follow-up. For 47 cases information was obtained
from other hospitals, public health officers or relatives. For 2 patients the
outcome classification was based on a questionnaire combined with other information.

The chronic hallucinatory schizophrenias correspond to a large extent to
the chronic hallucinatory psychoses of French authors (Ey, 1959). In Kraepelin's system (1910) it would be dementia paranoides mitis. Such psychoses represent a nosological problem group, and there may be doubt whether they
should be classified as schizophrenias.

At follow-up 88 patients were classified as severely deteriorated paranoid
schizophrenias. These psychoses are all clear-cut schizophrenias with marked
dissolution and splitting of personality. In a series of 306 unselected chronic

schizophrenias from Gaustad Hospital, patients with severe paranoid deterioration made up 18 per cent, nearly as many as those with slight paranoid defects (Astrup, 1962). In the present series they only made up 9 per cent, as compared with 51 per cent for the slight paranoid defects. This means that in a hospital population of chronic schizophrenics, the severe cases accumulate over the years, while they are comparatively rare in a series of consecutive first admissions to a mental hospital.

The 88 patients are sub-classified into confabulatory, expansive, fantastic and incoherent paraphrenias. In the total follow-up material the vast majority of the patients were seen personally in their homes. Only 11 of the severely deteriorated paraphrenias have been seen in their homes. Forty-two were at Gaustad Hospital at the time of re-examination, ten were in other mental hospitals, and 25 were under other types of psychiatric care. Apparently such patients can seldom live in their home surroundings. Only one of the patients seen at home was able to support himself by working at a job. The others were dependent upon relatives and social security pensions.

The catatonic schizophrenics could be subdivided into two major groups of 96 periodic, and 71 systematic, catatonias. Altogether 105 patients were personally re-examined. For 56 cases the clinical outcome was evaluated on the basis of records from other hospitals and public health officers.

Information was obtained from relatives and questionnaires for six patients. These six were all classified as periodic catatonias.

In a chronic hospital population (Astrup, 1962) there was a great predominance of systematic (31 per cent) over periodic (6 per cent) catatonias.

The slightly deteriorated hebephrenics comprised 35 cases with autistic and 118 cases with eccentric hebephrenia. We re-examined 57 patients in their homes and 23 at Gaustad Hospital. For 15 patients information about outcome was obtained from other hospitals, and for 53 from public health officers or relatives (mainly patients under psychiatric care). Five patients living outside the area selected for personal re-examination answered questionnaires, and additional information was provided by public health officers.

The severely deteriorated schizophrenics comprised 54 cases with shallow, and 28 cases with silly, hebephrenia. Six patients were seen in their homes, and 34 at Gaustad Hospital at the time of the re-examination. Twenty-three were in other psychiatric hospitals. For 19 patients information was obtained from public health officers (mainly patients under psychiatric care).

In the following chapters the characteristics of the above mentioned seven major subgroups of chronic schizophrenia will be described in more detail. The distribution of the coded clinical items at first admission will be shown for the various subgroups of chronic schizophrenia. Out of the 53 clinical factors with 2 to 11 subspecifications, only the most important clinical information has been picked out for this analysis. By comparing the coded clinical characteristics we can show to what extent the various types of chronic schizophrenias differ or can be distinguished from each other already at the onset of the illness. Relating these findings to the symptomatology in the chronic stages may give an impression of the dynamics of symptom formation.

IV. ATYPICAL PARANOID SCHIZOPHRENIA

a. Affect-laden paraphrenia

The outstanding feature of affect-laden paraphrenia is that the paranoid delusions have a strong affective loading. This is usually not the case in other types
of chronic paranoid schizophrenia. Leonhard (1966) points out that some cases
develop expansive and fantastic delusions with hallucinations in all sensory
fields. In the present author's experience such cases lose the affective loading
of delusions and cannot easily be separated from the typical paranoid schizophrenias. They have therefore been classified within the typical groups. The
material contains, however, the circumscribed delusional states with grandiose
delusions and strong affective loading, corresponding to Kraepelin's paranoia.
There are differential diagnostic problems as to the chronic hallucinatory types
of schizophrenia. In the present study patients are classified in the latter groups,
even if they are much affectively concerned with their chronic hallucinatory experiences. Accordingly, hallucinations are, as a rule, absent in the chronic
stages of the present material.

At the initial stages depression and elation frequently occur. Later on these
traits are not a regular part of the clinical picture, but may appear during exacerbations of the psychotic symptoms. The course of illness varies considerably. As a rule, there is a progressive development.

Many cases show fairly good remissions and later develop chronic paranoid
states. In other cases there may come an "encapsulation" of psychotic ideas
with the years. The patients are still convinced of the reality of their delusions,
lack insight and become rather upset when their delusions are discussed. But
they have learned that the more they keep their morbid ideas to themselves,
the less trouble they get with other people. We have even late remissions.
Thus, in several cases followed-up in 1956 and re-examined in 1966, the
schizophrenic symptomatology had faded away.

Psychotropic drugs are, as a rule, quite effective in reducing the affective loading of the delusions, but it seems that drug treatment must be maintained for a prolonged period to achieve lasting improvement (Astrup & Fish, 1964).

Patients with affect-laden paraphrenia as a rule have intact personalities, fairly good affective contact, and are rarely autistic. In discussions of their delusions they may be illogical and ramble on incomprehensibly, but their verbal communication on neutral topics is usually adequate. Mostly they have a good working capacity.

Fish (1958, 1964) and Astrup (1962) being unable to distinguish the subgroups as sharply as Leonhard, found often transitional forms between the 19 subgroups and classified such psychoses in the subgroups which most resembled on another. The present series is quite uniform in symptomatology centering around the delusions and the abnormal affect, as cases with typical schizophrenia have been excluded. It is evident that this group of schizophrenia is rather different from the nuclear dementia praecox. Even after prolonged observation periods doubt often arises whether the patients present non-schizophrenic states.

b. Schizophasia

Leonhard's (1966) concept of schizophasia is considerably wider than that of Kraepelin. He emphasizes that the essential feature of this subgroup is a breakdown of speech and thought, and he also uses the term "cataphasia". This type of psychosis occurs both in excited and inhibitory forms. The excited patients speak very much, while the inhibited patients speak very little. He also described mute patients in this group, but such cases are not included in the present material. The very few mute schizophrenic patients in our followup series have been classified as catatonics. The reason for this is that the psychomotor disturbances are marked, while speech confusion cannot be elicited.

In the easily recognizable cases of schizophasia there is a gross confusion of speech and even neologisms. This contrasts very much with the well ordered behaviour and good affective contact. Indications of delusions and hallucinations occur, but the speech distortions make it difficult to assess the presence of such symptoms.

The course of illness shows numerous remissions and exacerbations. In the tendency to fluctuations the schizophasias resemble affect-laden paraphrenia. Some cases have only slight speech disturbances and express delu-

sions and hallucinations periodically. Here it may be difficult to distinguish
the two types of atypical paranoid schizophrenia. There appears to be a transitional group with both affect-laden delusions and breakdown of speech and
thought. Neuroleptic drugs diminish both the affective loading of delusions and
the speech and thought distortions of schizophasia (Astrup & Fish, 1964). Thus
patients under drug treatment present a great differential diagnostic problem.
The schizophasias may also resemble catatonic cases with marked psychomotor disturbances in the acute stages, as well as during exacerbations. The
general principle has been to include in the schizophasic group all transitional
cases where the schizophasic breakdown of speech and thought can be ascertained.

In the mildest forms of schizophasia the patients can have a consistent conversation, but slip from time to time into unusual use of words, speak with
many grammatical mistakes, lose the logical connection between the sentences,
express themselves vaguely and scarcely comprehensibly, or become directly
incoherent. In such cases detailed follow-up information is needed in order to
secure a correct classification. It may even be difficult to distinguish these
cases from the milder defects of systematic type, especially when the patients
are treated with psychotropic drugs.

c. Coded clinical items

Among the 230 cases with affect-laden paraphrenia, there were 77 male and 153
female patients. We have thus a marked predominance of the female sex.
Schizophasia is more common in the male sex with 71 men and 48 female. In
our total material of followed-up patients with schizophrenic defects, there
are slightly more men than women. Affect-laden paraphrenia is accordingly
very atypical for our schizophrenic population with regard to sex distribution.
The hospital diagnoses at first admission are seen from table 8.

In affect-laden paraphrenia only 37 per cent received an initial diagnosis
of schizophrenia (83 per cent in the systematic schizophrenias). The most
frequent diagnosis was reactive paranoid psychosis. Altogether 51 per cent
received a hospital diagnosis of reactive psychosis (24 per cent in total series
of schizophrenics.) This means that the psychoses were presumed to occur
in deviating personalities in connection with external stress, and in particular
with psychological conflicts. A hospital diagnosis of manic-depressive psychosis has rarely been associated with schizophrenic outcome (2 per cent in

Table 8   Discharge diagnosis of the hospital

Outcome	Schizo-phrenia	Schizo-phrenia?	Reactive psychoses			Manic-depressive
			Depressive	Paranoid	Hysteric and confusional	
Affect-laden paraphrenia	37%	6%	7%	40%	4%	6%
Schizophasia	66%	8%	3%	14%	8%	2%
Total schizophrenic population	69%	6%	5%	15%	4%	2%

total series of schizophrenias). When this has been the case, revisions have mainly been in the direction of affect-laden paraphrenia.

Schizophasia shows a hospital diagnosis of schizophrenia in 66 per cent. This lies close to the average of our schizophrenic population (69 per cent).

The coding of premorbid personality is seen from table 9.

Table 9 Prepsychotic personality

Outcome	Schizoid	Sensi-tive	Self-asser-tive	Cycloid	Hysteri-cal	Neu-rotic	Asocial	Harmo-nious	Incom-plete infor-mation
Affect- laden paraphrenia	17%	20%	34%	2%	1%	4%	4%	13%	6%
Schizophasia	28%	23%	18%	1%	2%	3%	6%	13%	8%
Total schizophrenic population	38%	17%	16%	1%	1%	3%	6%	11%	7%

Self-assertive and sensitive premorbid personalities predominate in affect-laden paraphrenia. Such personality traits are found in 54 per cent and could very well be presumed to give a predisposition for paranoid reactions. Only 17 per cent had schizoid personalities as against 38 per cent in our total schizophrenic population. The schizophasic group has also many cases with sensitive and self-assertive personalities, but the self-assertive personalities are comparatively more common in affect-laden paraphrenia. 28 per cent have schizoid personalities, so that schizophasia in this respect comes closer to the average schizophrenic population.

The coding of precipitating factors is shown in table 10. Often there is a

Table 10

Outcome	Acute mental trauma	Prolonged mental conflicts		Social misery isolation	Somatic disease childbirth	Intoxication mostly alcoholic	No special factors mentioned
		Sexual	Others				
Affect-laden paraphrenia	7%	24%	32%	3%	13%	3%	32%
Schizophasia	6%	29%	30%	3%	12%	9%	32%
Total schizophrenic population	6%	20%	23%	3%	10%	5%	45%

combination of several factors, and in such cases only the two most important ones are coded (Astrup & Noreik, 1966). Two items are also coded in tables 11, 12, 13 and 14.

With regard to precipitating factors the two forms of atypical paranoid schizophrenias do not differ much from each other. In most cases some type of external precipitation is found. Lack of precipitating factors (32 per cent) is more common in our total schizophrenic population (45 per cent). The precipitating factors are predominantly prolonged mental conflicts, while acute mental trauma rarely has been coded.

The distribution of affective traits at the onset is seen from table 11.

Nearly one-half of the patients with affect-laden paraphrenia have depression,

Table 11 Affective traits

Outcome	Depression	Elation, eu-phoria, ecstasy	Perplexity	Anxiety	Affective instability	Emotional blunting
Affect-laden paraphrenia	46%	26%	17%	12%	41%	10%
Schizophasia	27%	45%	24%	7%	25%	29%
Total schizo-phrenic population	29%	22%	20%	8%	27%	44%

which is markedly more frequent than in our total schizophrenic population (29 per cent). Also, affective instability is more common (41 per cent, as compared with 27 per cent). This included rage, irritation and "impure" affect, and is mainly coded in paranoid psychoses without other affective traits. Emotional blunting is only found in 10 per cent, but is present in 44 per cent of our total schizophrenic population.

Schizophasia has very often elation, ecstasy or euphoria in the initial stages (45 per cent as compared with 22 per cent in the total schizophrenic population). Depression and affective instability are about as frequent as in the other schizophrenic subgroups, but emotional blunting is only coded in 29 per cent of the cases.

Table 12 surveys the types of delusions. We have defined megalomania, fantasy lover, ideas of high descent and fantastic ideas of jealousy as typical schizophrenic delusions, because these delusions are especially associated with long-term schizophrenic outcome.

In both types of atypical paranoid schizophrenia absence of delusions is rare at the initial stage. The typical schizophrenic delusions are more often found than in our total schizophrenic population. Megalomanic delusions are especially frequent in schizophasia. Persecution mania is present in 71 per cent during the initial stages, but occurs as often as in 59 per cent of our total schizophrenic population.

The types of disturbance of thinking are shown in table 13. Here we have defined depersonalization, passivity and symbolism as typical schizophrenic

Table 12   Delusional content

Outcome	Guilt in-feriority	Hypo-chon-dria	Ideas of refer-ence	Perse-cution-mania	Revin-dica-tion	Megalomania		Fantacy lover	Ideas of high descent	Fantastic ideas of jealousy	No delu-sions estab-lished
						Reli-gious	Other forms				
Affect-laden paraphrenia	8%	6%	25%	76%	5%	10%	6%	6%	4%	16%	1&
Schizophasia	6%	9%	16%	61%	3%	20%	18%	13%	5%	10%	5%
Total schizo-phrenic population	6%	10%	24%	59%	2%	11%	9%	7%	4%	7%	14%

Table 13   Disturbance of thinking

Outcome	Flight of ideas	Incoherence	Depersonali-sation	Passivity	Symbolism	No mention of thought dis-turbance
Affect-laden paraphrenia	2%	7%	30%	44%	66%	13%
Schizophasia	1%	27%	47%	50%	51%	4%
Total schizophrenic population	1%	19%	39%	50%	41%	13%

thought disorders.

In both groups there is mostly coded thought disturbance. Incoherence is comparatively frequent in schizophasia, but the thought confusion of these patients can be traced back to the initial stages of the psychosis in only 27 per cent of the cases. The typical schizophrenic thought disturbances are about as frequent as in our total schizophrenic population. It is noted that depersonal-ization is more common in schizophasia, while symbolism is especially char-acteristic of affect-laden paraphrenia. In the latter group there are, as a rule, from the onset systematized delusions with symbolic interpretations.

The types of hallucinations are seen from table 14. Haptic and special forms of auditory hallucinations have been defined as typically schizophrenic. The haptic hallucinations are usually ascribed to some type of external influence from rays, electricity, etc. The special forms of auditory hallucinations include hearing of thoughts, conversation with voices, voices with comments on the patient's movements and voices coming from the patient's own head or body.

Table 14   Hallucinations

Outcome	Auditory	Auditory special forms	Olfactory gustatory	Visual	Haptic		Without hallu- cination
					Sexual	Others	
Affect-laden paraphrenia	61%	10%	10%	12%	7%	25%	22%
Schizophasia	66%	23%	8%	17%	7%	30%	13%
Total schizophrenic population	68%	19%	7%	14%	7%	26%	15%

In both groups of psychoses the typical schizophrenic hallucinations occur as often as in other types of schizophrenic defects. The special forms of auditory hallucinations are, however, comparatively rare in affect-laden paraphrenia. In this group there are also many cases without hallucinations at the onset. In such cases the psychotic symptoms are from the beginning centered around the affect-laden delusions.

The age of onset of psychotic symptoms is seen from table 15.

Affect-laden paraphrenia has a marked tendency to start late in life. Also schizophasia starts later than in the typical schizophrenic subgroups. Onset at 20 or below is rarely seen in these types of psychoses.

The duration of psychotic symptoms before admission is illustrated by table 16.

Here the two types of atypical paranoid schizophrenia do not differ much from each other. Compared with our total schizophrenic population there are also small differences. Prolonged duration before admission appears to occur

Table 15   Age at onset

Outcome	20 years or less	21 – 30 years	31 – 40 years	40 years
Affect-laden paraphrenia	0%	13%	31%	55%
Schizophasia	4%	27%	43%	26%
Total schizophrenic population	10%	34%	29%	27%

Table 16   Duration of illness before admission

Outcome	$\frac{1}{2}$ year	$\frac{1}{2}$ – 1 years	1 – 2 years	2 – 5 years	5-10 years	10 years
Affect-laden paraphrenia	27%	7%	16%	24%	12%	15%
Schizophasia	29%	8%	16%	24%	14%	9%
Total schizophrenic population	27%	7%	15%	24%	14%	12%

because of the slight defects, which allow social adjustment in spite of psychotic symptoms. In the cases with a duration of less than six months, the differential diagnosis against non-schizophrenic psychoses is especially difficult. The main reason for this are the affective disturbances with marked depressive or elated features.

The distribution of psychomotor symptoms shows that blocking, stupor, excitation and mannerisms are more often found in the schizophasic, than in affect-laden cases. This shows that these cases initially often resemble psychoses with a catatonic outcome.

The initial symptoms do not reveal many differences. It is noted that change of personality, which is prognostically very unfavourable, rarely occurs in affect-laden paraphrenia (6 per cent), quite often in schizophasia (24 per cent), but not as often in our total schizophrenic population (35 per cent).

The clinical syndromes at the onset have been coded.

Affect-laden paraphrenia, more often than typical schizophrenias, has a syndrome of depression, while hebephrenic (3 per cent) and catatonic (3 per cent) syndromes are rare at the onset. Each of the latter syndromes are coded in 12 per cent of the schizophasic cases. The paranoid syndromes are coded in 92 per cent of the atypical paranoid psychoses at the onset.

Intelligence below average is more frequent in schizophasia (22 per cent) than in affect-laden paraphrenia (14 per cent), and occurs in 16 per cent of our total schizophrenic population.

Both types of psychoses have very similar types of onset, and as often insidious onset as in the total schizophrenic population.

About one-half of the cases have an observation period of less than 10 years since first admission. This does not differ from the average in our series of schizophrenic patients. The tendency to slight defects thus apparently does not show that the patients have been followed up for shorter periods than other schizophrenic cases.

d. Discussion

With regard to symptom coding at first admission, several differences can be found between the atypical paranoid schizophrenias and our total population of followed-up patients with schizophrenic defects. For most of the coded items the differences are moderate, and there are no indications of pathognomonic symptoms or sharp delimitations. Accordingly, the clinical factors analyzed in the present study have a rather limited value for predicting an atypical schizophrenic courses of illness. Schizophasia is less atypical than affect-laden paraphrenia. Hospital diagnosis at first admission has, as a rule, been schizophrenia. Typical schizophrenic delusions, thought disturbances, and hallucinations are as frequent as in the typical schizophrenic subgroups.

However, there are fewer ones with schizoid personalities, precipitating factors are most found, and the affective disturbances go more in the direction of elation than of emotional blunting. This type of schizophrenia is mainly atypical insofar as the course of illness often shows remissions and exacerbations. Furthermore, the defects tend to be mild at re-examination. For the milder defects, it may sometimes be difficult to determine whether the defect is schizophrenic or a residual of a reactive or atypical manic-depressive psychosis. In particular doubts may arise as to whether the clinical state at re-examination represents personality changes of a non-schizophrenic paranoid state.

Affect-laden paraphrenia is clearly different from the typical schizophrenias already from the onset of the illness. This type of psychosis is predominantly found in the female sex. It may well be that this reflects a general tendency of female patients to be more affectively involved with their symptoms than male patients, but may also imply more resemblance to the catamnestically verified reactive and manic-depressive psychoses, which were most common in the female sex (Astrup, et al., 1962).

Premorbid personalities are mostly self-assertive and sensitive, while schizoid personalities are rare. Precipitating factors are found as a rule, mainly in the form of prolonged mental conflicts. These circumstances can probably explain that the most frequent hospital diagnosis has been reactive psychosis, and in particular of paranoid type. Sensitive and self-assertive personalities are especially predisposed to paranoid reactions. We have, however, the problem that what we code as premorbid personality in some cases may be personality changes resulting from a long-lasting paranoid development. With regard to precipitating factors, it is sometimes difficult to determine to what extent the conflicts actually precede the psychosis, or whether the prodromes of the psychosis bring the patients into conflicts with their environment. When the case history shows that the latter is the case, absence of precipitating factors has always been coded.

Compared with a series of 206 catamnestically verified reactive psychoses (Astrup, et al., 1962) the affect-laden paraphrenias have comparatively more self-assertive, less sensitive, hysterical and neurotic premorbid personalities. Acute mental trauma is more frequent and absence of precipitating factors less frequent in the reactive psychoses. Accordingly, affect-laden paraphrenia differs considerably both from reactive psychoses as a group, and from the typical schizophrenias with regard to personality traits and precipitating factors.

Like the reactive and manic-depressive psychoses, affect-laden paraphrenia has a large proportion with depressive features, and they differ from the other types of schizophrenia with much less emotional blunting and change of personality as initial symptoms.

Typical schizophrenic delusions, thought disturbances, and hallucinations are about as common as in other types of catamnestically verified schizophrenias. Persecutory delusions are most frequent in the acute stage, and also predominate in the chronic stages. Ideas of reference belong mainly to the acute stages. We have a few cases with chronic sensitive delusions of reference, corresponding to the "Beziehungswahn" of Kretschmer (1927), but these are not included in our group of affect-laden paraphrenia.

Megalomanic delusions and ideas of high descent are mainly seen in the acute stages, while revindication, fantastic ideas of jealousy and fantasy lover tend to persist.

Disturbance of thinking is predominantly symbolism. This reflects that the onset tends to be characterized by systematized delusions along with symbolic interpretations. The symbolic distortions persist, and even often progress during the chronic stages. The other types of thought disturbances are only found in the initial stages and during psychotic exacerbations.

Hallucinations as a rule occur in the acute stages. Later they disappear, but may reappear in periods with worsening of the clinical condition.

The age of onset is very high, corresponding much more to that of our reactive and manic-depressive psychoses than our typical schizophrenias. The high age of onset is thus associated with the tendency to rather circumscribed paranoid psychoses with mild defects.

With regard to duration of illness, the affect-laden paraphrenias have few cases of short duration. These acute psychoses resemble very much the atypical endogenous psychoses, which Leonhard (1966) calls anxiety- ecstasy psychoses. The mild defects probably explain that many patients with affect-laden paraphrenia have rather delayed admissions. Our catamnestically verified reactive and manic-depressive psychoses as a rule have less than six months duration prior to admission. Thus, the duration of illness is an important factor for the differential diagnosis between these psychoses and affect-laden paraphrenia.

Although the atypical paranoid schizophrenias in several ways differ from other types of schizophrenia, the author thinks they should be included in the group of schizophrenias. The psychoses start with typical schizophrenic delusions, thought disturbances and hallucinations as often as the typical schizophrenias. They also develop chronic defect states which are different from the residuals of catamnestically verified manic-depressive and reactive psychoses. In the latter a chronic psychotic development is rare, but the rule in atypical paranoid schizophrenia.

V. CHRONIC HALLUCINATORY SCHIZOPHRENIAS

a. Phonemic paraphrenia

These psychoses usually start out as paranoid hallucinatory psychoses. In the chronic stage verbal hallucinosis is the most characteristic symptom. Often the voices make comments on the patient's thoughts and previous life experiences. They talk about things which are unpleasant and disturbing. The patient may, for instance, be accused of having a low sexual morality, behaving badly in other ways, or being dangerous for the community. In other cases the voices may be making friendly and hostile comments on the patient's life. The patients may also talk to the voices. Often they believe that the voices come from persons around them, and may then be angry and complain.

The affect is usually neutral, may be euphoric or slightly blunted, but not depressive, even if they complain about accusations from the voices. The defect is slight, and most patients have a good working capacity.

Drugs make the hallucinations less distressing, but do not remove them (Astrup & Fish, 1964). Thus the chronic hallucinatory psychoses have a great tendency to persist, and they can, as a rule, be well recognized, even if the patients are under drug treatment. Over the years some patients care less about the voices, but one rarely sees a disappearance corresponding to the late remissions with "encapsulation" of delusions.

In our series of patients there are a number of variations in symptomatology. Some patients hear the voices practically every day, others periodically. The voices may come from the body as well as from outside. Voices may be heard in only one ear. A few patients relate that their thoughts are repeated, so that everybody knows what they think. The voices may also be felt as speech movements. The majority of the cases with phonemic paraphrenia became so accustomed to their voices that at re-examination they cared less about them than they did at admission.

In the present series 37 patients were hospitalized at the time of the follow-up, and quite many of them have later been discharged. Forty-one cases were personally seen in their homes. All but six were self-supporting, but most of them less stable in work than before their illness started. This suggests that it is possible for patients with phonemic paraphrenia to make a good adjustment in the community.

Altogether 75 patients had manifest chronic hallucinosis at the time of the follow-up. In 15 cases the hallucinations occurred so rarely that the patients were classified as improved with schizophrenic personality changes.

b. Hypochondriacal paraphrenia

The central symptoms of this group are combinations of auditory and bodily hallucinations. The patients often tell about being exposed to electrical currents or rays. They may complain about being sexually misused, or that the brain, spinal chord, stomach or other internal organs are damaged by machines and rays. The hypochondriacal sensations are often very bizarre.

The voices are usually disconnected phrases, and not complete sentences as in phonemic paraphrenia. Sometimes the voices comment on what the patients think and do. The voices may also utter commands or accusations. The patient can be called a "louse", a "homosexual", or a "spy", but this is not discussed and set in relation to his life experiences. The patients complain mainly about the voices, but care less about the content which has a less intimate character than in phonemic paraphrenia.

The patients do not attribute voices and hypochondriacal sensations to persons around them. They may say that some unknown persons or organizations are responsible for their sufferings, but do not develop systematized delusions.

There is usually a slight blunting of affect. The patients tend to be depressed, irritable, discontent and complain that they suffer very much from the voices and the bodily hallucinations. Even in long-standing psychoses patients state that their thoughts are under external control. This passivity is not seen in other type of chronic schizophrenia.

The most important feature distinguishing them from phonemic paraphrenia is the presence of hypochondriacal sensations. The character of the voices and the depressive and irritable mood also differentiate this syndrome. Other types of chronic schizophrenia rarely give differential diagnostic problems.

The patients have slight defects and are, as a rule, good and trustworthy workers. Phenothiazines reduce the intensity of the symptoms, but are less effective than for phonemic paraphrenia (Astrup & Fish, 1964).

As a rule these patients are practically unchanged over very prolonged observation periods, and the hallucinatory experiences have often the same character as in the initial stages of the illness.

Patients with hypochondriacal paraphrenia give less occasion for discussion whether they should be included in the group of schizophrenias than phonemic paraphrenia. The main reason for this may be the multiple symptomatology, with both auditory and haptic hallucinations. Their personalities are, however, about as well preserved. In the present series 31 were hospitalized at follow-up, but many have been discharged later. Sixteen patients re-examined in their homes had a fairly good social adaptation. The need for prolonged hospital treatment appears to be less determined by the clinical condition than by social and personal factors.

In 57 patients the chronic hallucinatory state was present at follow-up. Four cases had only episodical hallucinations and were classified as improved with schizophrenic personality changes. The chronicity of symptomatology is more pronounced than in phonemic paraphrenia.

c. Coded clinical items

Among patients with phonemic paraphrenia there were 39 men and 51 women, whereas there were 35 males and 26 female patients with hypochondriacal paraphrenia. Thus, the two types of psychoses show a slight difference with regard to sex distribution.

The hospital diagnoses at first admission are seen from Table 17.

Table 17

Outcome	Discharge diagnosis of the hospital					Total cases
			Reactive psychoses			
	Schizophrenia	Schizophrenia?	Depressive	Paranoid	Hysteric and confusional	
Phonemic paraphrenia	62 %	7 %	7 %	14 %	10 %	90
Hypochondriacal paraphrenia	77 %	3 %	0 %	18 %	2 %	61
Total schizophrenic population	69 %	6 %	5 %	15 %	4 %	990

No case received a diagnosis of manic-depressive psychosis, which occurred several times in the atypical paranoid schizophrenias. The main differential diagnosis at discharge is towards reactive psychoses. A diagnosis of schizophrenia is used in 62 per cent of the phonemic and 77 per cent of the hypochondriacal paraphrenias. The latter groups shows, accordingly, more clearcut schizophrenia from the beginning.

The coding of premorbid personality is seen from Table 18.

Table 18

Outcome	Prepsychotic personality									
	Schizoid	Sensitive	Self-assertive	Cycloid	Hysterical	Neurotic	Epileptoid	Asocial	Harmonious	Incomplete information
Phonemic paraphrenia	29 %	27 %	12 %	3 %	3 %	1 %	0 %	9 %	11 %	4 %
Hypochondriacal paraphrenia	46 %	15 %	21 %	0 %	0 %	2 %	2 %	5 %	10 %	0 %
Total schizophrenic population	38 %	17 %	16 %	1 %	1 %	3 %	0 %	6 %	11 %	7 %

Schizoid personalities are most frequent, and the occurence corresponds to the average for our schizophrenic population (38%). In particular, many of the cases with hypochondriacal paraphrenia have this type of personality. Sensitive personalities are often found in phonemic paraphrenia, while the hypochondriacal cases have more self-assertive personalities.

Precipitating factors are seen from Table 19.

Outcome	Precipitating factors						
	Acute mental trauma	Prolonged mental conflicts		Social misery, isolation	Somatic disease childbirth	Intoxication, mostly alcoholic	No special factors mentioned
		Sexual	Others				
Phonemic paraphrenia	6 %	34 %	23 %	3 %	7 %	9 %	38 %
Hypochondriacal paraphrenia	2 %	26 %	23 %	2 %	10 %	5 %	48 %
Total schizophrenic population	6 %	20 %	23 %	3 %	10 %	5 %	45 %

Hypochondriacal paraphrenia has many cases with no precipitating factors (48%). When precipitating factors are coded, there are predominantly pro-longed mental conflicts in both groups. It is difficult here to determine to what extent the conflicts actually have precipitated the psychoses, or the beginning psychosis has brought the patients trouble.

The distribution of affective traits is seen from Table 20.

Table 20

Outcome	Affective traits					
	Depression	Elation, euphoria, ecstasy	Perplexity	Anxiety	Affective instability	Emotional blunting
Phonemic paraphrenia	32 %	20 %	17 %	10 %	24 %	38 %
Hypochondriacal paraphrenia	34 %	16 %	16 %	3 %	38 %	39 %
Total schizophrenic population	29 %	22 %	20 %	8 %	27 %	44 %

Emotional blunting has been present in many cases from the onset, and this distinguishes the chronic hallucinatory psychoses from the atypical paranoid schizophrenias (Astrup, 1969), 17%). (P < .001). This symptom is more com-mon in our total schizophrenic population. However, the majority of the cases start with other emotional symptoms. Depressive or elated mood at the initial stages has essentially no value in predicting which kind of defect will develop.

Table 21 surveys the types of delusions.

Table 21

Outcome	Delusional content										
	Guilt inferio-rity	Hypo-chon-dria	Ideas of refe-rence	Perse-cution	Revin-dica-tion	Megalomania		Fanta-sy lover	Ideas of high descent	Fantastic ideas of jealousy	No delusions established
						Reli-gious	Other forms				
Phonemic paraphrenia	4 %	8 %	31 %	76 %	2 %	12 %	6 %	8 %	2 %	9 %	6 %
Hypo-chondriacal paraphrenia	2 %	18 %	36 %	89 %	2 %	3 %	3 %	13 %	2 %	3 %	2 %
Total schizophrenic population	6 %	10 %	24 %	59 %	2 %	11 %	9 %	7 %	4 %	7 %	14 %

In practically all cases delusions have been recorded at the initial stage of the illness. Most frequent is persecution, and next ideas of reference. Hypochondriacal delusions are rare. They dominate the chronic stage of hypochondriacal paraphrenia, but in the initial stages the symptoms have been coded as haptic hallucinations more often than as elaborated delusions.

The types of disturbance of thinking are seen from Table 22.

Table 22

Outcome	Disturbance of thinking				
	Incoherence	Depersonalization	Passivity	Symbolism	No mention of thought disturbance
Phonemic paraphrenia	7 %	47 %	74 %	53 %	3 %
Hypochondriacal paraphrenia	7 %	46 %	85 %	46 %	3 %
Total schizophrenic population	19 %	39 %	50 %	41 %	13 %

Absence of thought disturbance is rare. No case showed flight of ideas and very few had incoherence. Depersonalization, passivity and symbolism have been defined by us as typical schizophrenic thought disorders (Astrup & Noreik, 1966). The chronic hallucinatory psychoses are characterized by a massive occurrence of such symptoms at the onset. They have more such symptoms than any of the other schizophrenic subgroups. Passivity predominates, especially in hypochondriacal paraphrenia.

The types of hallucinations are seen from Table 23.

It is noted that practically all cases have had hallucinations from the onset of the psychosis. Hypochoncriacal paraphrenia has more haptic hallucinations which are found always at follow-up (P $<$ .001). Phonemic paraphrenia has comparatively more of the special forms of auditory hallucinations, which often persist in the chronic stages (P $<$ .001). These include hearing one's own thoughts, conversation with voices, voices which comment on the patient's movements, and voices coming from the patient's own head or body.

The age of onset of the psychosis is seen from Table 24.

The two types of psychoses do not differ much from each other with regard to age of onset. Very few develop in the youngest age group, and the majority

Table 23

Outcome	Hallucinations						
	Auditory	Auditory Special forms	Olfactory, gustatory	Visual	Haptic		Without hallucination
					Sexual	Others	
Phonemic paraphrenia	88 %	41 %	8 %	12 %	6 %	24 %	1 %
Hypochondriacal paraphrenia	71 %	30 %	8 %	5 %	16 %	51 %	2 %
Total schizophrenic population	68 %	19 %	7 %	14 %	7 %	25 %	15 %

Table 24

Outcome	Age at onset			
	20 years or less	21 - 30 years	31 - 40 years	40 years
Phonemic paraphrenia	2 %	28 %	33 %	37 %
Hypochondriacal paraphrenia	5 %	28 %	34 %	33 %
Total schizophrenic population	10 %	34 %	29 %	27 %

above 30. Compared with most other types of schizophrenia, age of onset is rather high.

The duration of psychotic symptoms at admission is seen from Table 25.

Several cases have a short duration of illness, and the problem in such cases has been mainly the differential diagnosis with reactive psychoses. There are also a number of cases with prolonged duration of more than 5 years. Duration of illness is not essentially different from that of the total

Table 25

Outcome	Duration of illness before admission					
	< ½ year	½ - 1 year	1 - 2 years	2 - 5 years	5 - 10 years	> 10 years
Phonemic paraphrenia	26 %	6 %	19 %	29 %	10 %	11 %
Hypochondriacal paraphrenia	30 %	8 %	11 %	26 %	16 %	8 %
Total schizophrenic population	27 %	7 %	15 %	24 %	14 %	12 %

Table 26

Outcome	Psychomotor symptoms								
	Inhibition	Blocking	Stupor	Excitation	Mannerism	Agitation Restlessness	Negativism	Varying	No psychomotor disturbances mentioned
Phonemic paraphrenia	13 %	17 %	4 %	24 %	9 %	8 %	6 %	1 %	39 %
Hypochondriacal paraphrenia	5 %	8 %	0 %	15 %	8 %	11 %	10 %	5 %	54 %
Total schizophrenic population	9 %	20 %	7 %	28 %	13 %	8 %	9 %	2 %	36 %

schizophrenic population.

The psychomotor symptoms at onset are shown in Table 26.

Hypochondriacal paraphrenia has comparatively more cases without psychomotor symptoms, while phonemic paraphrenia has more with inhibition, blocking and excitation. Stupor and mannerisms are quite rare in both groups.

The initial symptoms are seen from Table 27.

It is noted that more than one-half have a typical paranoid onset with ideas

Table 27

Outcome	Initial symptoms								
	Transitory periods	Change of personality	Depressive traits	Neurasthenic traits	Ideas of reference suspicious jealous	Impulsive tantrums	Vagrancy restlessness	Religious or philosophical preoccupation	No special initial symptoms mentioned
Phonemic paraphrenia	23 %	31 %	17 %	14 %	52 %	8 %	3 %	2 %	0 %
Hypochondriacal paraphrenia	13 %	23 %	10 %	8 %	69 %	2 %	3 %	0 %	7 %
Total schizophrenic population	15 %	35 %	12 %	11 %	47 %	12 %	4 %	5 %	3 %

of reference, suspiciousness or jealousy. Change of personality is considerably more rare than in cases developing severe paranoid deterioration (42%), (P < .005), and not as common as in the total schizophrenic population (35%). The clinical syndromes at onset are found in Table 28.

Table 28

Outcome	Clinical syndrome at onset						
	Depression	Excitation	Confusion	Paranoid	Hebephrenic	Catatonic	Hysteriform
Phonemic paraphrenia	18 %	7 %	7 %	92 %	16 %	4 %	1 %
Hypochondriacal paraphrenia	3 %	0 %	2 %	98 %	15 %	2 %	0 %
Total schizophrenic population	11 %	5 %	3 %	78 %	29 %	19 %	1 %

As expected, the paranoid syndromes dominate from the beginning, although there are several cases with hebephrenic syndromes at the onset. A catatonic syndrome is rare. Depression, excitation, and confusion are noted mainly in phonemic paraphrenia, and about as frequent in this group as in the atypical paranoid schizophrenias.

The distribution of the coded intelligence follows from Table 29.

Table 29

Outcome	Intelligence		
	Incomplete information	Below average	Average or above
Phonemic paraphrenia	0 %	22 %	78 %
Hypochondriacal paraphrenia	0 %	18 %	82 %
Total schizophrenic population	1 %	22 %	77 %

The two groups are close to the average of our total schizophrenic population, and do not essentially differ from each other.

Types of onset are illustrated by Table 30.

Table 30

Outcome	Onset of disease				
	Acute onset without prodromal symptoms	Acute onset after prodromal symptoms	Sub-acute onset	Insidious onset with periodic exacerbations	Insidious onset without periodic exacerbations
Phonemic paraphrenia	16 %	13 %	22 %	29 %	20 %
Hypochondriacal paraphrenia	13 %	10 %	23 %	30 %	25 %
Total schizophrenic population	10 %	13 %	25 %	23 %	28 %

About one-half of the cases have an insidious onset, while the majority of cases with severe paranoid deterioration have such onset (60%). There are slightly more phonemic (29%) than hypochoncriacal cases (23%) with acute onset.

Table 31

Outcome	Body type			
	Incomplete information	Pyknic	Leptosome	Others or uncharacteristic
Phonemic paraphrenia	9 %	28 %	31 %	32 %
Hypochondriacal paraphrenia	5 %	10 %	49 %	36 %
Total schizophrenic population	5 %	19 %	39 %	36 %

Body types are shown in Table 31.

It is noted that pyknic body build is much rarer in hypochondriacal than in phonemic paraphrenia (P $<$ .05). For this finding, one must make the reservation that the coding of body type is based on clinical judgment without exact measurement.

The observation period since first admission is seen from Table 32.

Table 32

Outcome	Observation period since first admission		
	5 - 9 years	10 - 14 years	15 years or more
Phonemic paraphrenia	53 %	26 %	21 %
Hypochondriacal paraphrenia	39 %	33 %	28 %
Total schizophrenic population	47 %	29 %	24 %

Hypochondriacal paraphrenia tends to have a longer observation period than phonemic paraphrenia. This may indicate that hypochondriacal paraphrenia needs a longer time to develop the typical defect state. Duration of illness before admission was about the same in the two groups. (Table 25)

d. Discussion

At the initial stage of illness the two types of chronic hallucinatory psychoses do not distinguish themselves much from each other with regard to the coded clinical characteristics analyzed in the present study. The same was true for the sample of chronic mental hospital patients of the same two types (Astrup, 1962). Most of the clinical background factors also show the same distribution as for our total schizophrenic population.

There are some differential diagnostic problems with reactive psychoses at the onset, but less than in the atypical paranoid schizophrenias. Quite many have sensitive and self-assertive prepsychotic personalities, and precipitating factors are often coded. Several cases have also a short duration of illness. These circumstances will, at the onset, create differential diagnostic problems with reactive psychoses, which as a rule develop acutely in abnormal personalities in relation to external stress.

The affective traits are quite varied at the onset. Emotional blunting is more frequent than in the atypical paranoid schizophrenias (Astrup, 1969), but less frequent than in our total schizophrenic population. The affective traits at the onset give no indications that the mood in the chronic stages tends to develop in opposite directions, with phonemic paraphrenia showing a tendency to euphoria and hypochondriacal paraphrenia a tendency to a depressive, morose mood.

Very few cases have no delusions at admission. The various delusions observed at the onset disappear with chronic development. It is noted that persecution and ideas of reference are the most frequent types. In both types of psychoses, the schizophrenic thought disturbances play a central role at the initial stages, and feelings of passivity may even persist in the chronic stages of hypochondriacal paraphrenia.

Hallucinations are practically always found at the onset, but are distributed differently in the two groups. There are slightly more of the special forms of auditory hallucinations in phonemic paraphrenia, which often shows such symptoms in the chronic stages, in particular voices coming from the head or body. Hypochondriacal paraphrenia is characterized by haptic hallucinations, and many cases reveal such hallucinations in the beginning. On the other hand, several cases with phonemic paraphrenia have such symptoms initially, which later disappear.

Syndromes of depression, excitation and confusion are more frequent in phonemic paraphrenia (combined $P < .001$). This group also shows more psychomotor inhibition, blocking and excitation at onset (combined $P < .001$). In hypochondriacal paraphrenia a hospital diagnosis of schizophrenia on first admission is more frequent, more patients have schizoid personalities ($P < .05$), and the observation period is longer. All this suggests that hypochondriacal paraphrenia is more clear-cut from the onset as paranoid schizophrenia, and may need a longer time to develop the typical defect state.

Phonemic and hypochondriacal paraphrenia have sufficiently characteristic symptoms to be distinguished from other types of schizophrenic defects. This is also reflected in the French tradition of using the term chronic hallucinatory psychoses.

Pauleikhoff (1966) mentions that paranoid-hallucinatory psychoses developing in the fourth decade of life have a characteristic syndrome with prolonged course of illness of ten years or more. There is no personality deterioration, and by diagnosing these cases as schizophrenia, the specific features of the clinical condition are not sufficiently emphasized. Also, in our series, patients with phonemic and hypochondriacal paraphrenia have rather intact personalities, but they have more symptoms in common with the schizophrenic than with the reactive or manic-depressive psychoses. Some emotional blunting is usually present. As a rule their thinking shows vagueness.

Initiative and emotional contact are reduced, and autism is mostly present. To separate them from the schizophrenias would be no less justified than with many other of our schizophrenic subgroups with slight defects.

Age of onset tends to be higher than in most other schizophrenic subgroups. Thus these psychoses follow the general rule that onset at higher age is associated with slight defects in the chronic stages.

Although the symptom analysis gave small differences between phonemic and hypochondriacal paraphrenia, these psychoses may often be separated from each other already at admission, when the total clinical picture is evaluated. The symptom coding gives a crude quantitative measure, which shows their similarity. Differences of constellations of symptoms are better seen with a focused analysis of the more subtle clinical features in each individual case.

VI. THE SEVERELY DETERIORATED PARANOID SCHIZOPHRENIAS

a. Confabulatory paraphrenia

Fourteen patients were classified as belonging to this subgroup, ten male and four female. Confabulatory paraphrenia was described by Kraepelin (1910), but Leonhard has defined this group in more detail. The central symptomatology is here confabulation. The patients relate fantastic stories about their experiences. They may have travelled to far parts of the earth, even to the moon or the stars. The experiences may have occurred at other times, as in the Stone Age. Often patients relate having talked with kings or even with God. Vivid and detailed descriptions of the alleged events are given. Sometimes the patients may show critical attitudes to their experiences, tell that they happened in a kind of trance or dream-state, and thus could be distinguished from ordinary human experiences. It is also characteristic that the confabulations change from time to time, and mostly are forgotten when asked about later. The patients correctly evaluate their immediate surroundings. Although their confabulations have a fantastic and expansive character, the patients do not pose as important or superior persons. The mood is, as a rule, euphoric, and there is considerable emotional blunting. These patients have difficulties in carrying on an orderly conversation, and their working ability is slight. The total impression is one of severe deterioration, but less than in the other types of severe paranoid deterioration.

b. Expansive paraphrenia

Twenty-six patients were classified in this group, 15 men and 11 women. Kraepelin (1910) has described a type of expansive paraphrenia with such additional symptoms as hallucinations and persecutory delusions. Leonhard points out that the additional symptoms do not belong to the clinical picture in the chronic stages. He emphasizes also that this is the only pure delusional type among the typical or systematic schizophrenias.

The patients adopt a kind of haughty pose and take on a superior attitude when dealing with others. This can distinguish them from confabulatory and fantastic paraphrenics who also reveal expansive traits. Often the patients try to impress with their style of dress and high-sounding phrases.

The mood is euphoric and the affect is blunted. Verbal communication is as a rule poor, working capacity small, and the deterioration marked.

c. Fantastic paraphrenia

In this group, 38 patients were classified, 19 of each sex. These patients may have a very rich symptomatology, where a number of clinical phenomena tend to be combined. Expansive ideas are practically always present. The patient may for instance be the king of the Universe or God. There are somatic sensations, often of a grotesque and fantastic character. The patients may tell about animals passing through their body or living in their body. Internal organs may be torn out and replaced. Mass hallucinations are often reported. Thousands of people may be heard crying or seen murdered. Some patients complain about mass murder taking place in the basement or in other rooms. Individuals in the patient's environment are misidentified, and the patients regularly tell that they have met them previously under other names. Like patients with confabulatory paraphrenia, the fantastic paraphrenics often talk about travels to other countries, or even to the moon or stars. The borders between life and death vanish, and the limits of age, time and space disappear. Patients claim to have been dead, buried and restored to life. They say that they are millions of years old, and have lived in pre-historic times. Nature seems to be alive in these patients, so that birds, trees and inanimate objects speak to them.

In the author's experiences there are gradual transitions between the four types of severe paranoid defects. Expansive and confabulatory paraphrenias can be considered as more monosymptomatic forms, when compared with the fantastic cases. Often there is an incomplete symptom complex of fantastic paraphrenia, but when symptoms go beyond those properly belonging to the two former groups, patients are classified as fantastic paraphrenias. Incoherent paraphrenics have too poor a verbal communication to express the fantastic symptom complex, but may utter sentences suggesting some such features.

The fantastic patients can, as a rule, look after themselves, and many of

them can do routine work in the hospital. They have difficulties in carrying
out an ordered conversation, and their general behaviour shows more deterior&
tion than the monosymptomatic forms.

d. Incoherent paraphrenia

Only seven men and three women were classified as belonging to this group.
These patients are so confused that an ordered conversation is impossible.
In contrast to schizophasics, incoherent paraphrenics are disordered in gene-
ral behaviour as well as in speech.

Another central symptom is massive auditory hallucinosis. The patients
appear to be constantly conversing with voices. They may whisper, talk quiet-
ly or shout to the voices. Often they look at the walls or the ceiling, and make
gestures, as if discussing and quarreling with invisible people.

These patients pay little attention to the surroundings, seldom answer questions, have no initiative, and no interest in anything.

The incoherent paraphrenics have no working ability, and need help with
dressing, eating and cleanliness. They present one of the most severe types
of schizophrenic deterioration and correspond to dementia paranoides gravis
of Kraepelin (1910), or the "schizokare Verblödung" of Mauz (1930).

e. Coded clinical items

Among the severely deteriorated paranoid patients there were 51 men and 37
women. There is thus a slight preponderance of the male sex here, while
mild paranoid defects are more frequent in the female sex.   When divided
into subgroups fantastic paraphrenia is found with as many women as men.

The hospital diagnosis at first admission is seen in table 33.

These patients are from the beginning usually considered to be suffering
from schizophrenic psychoses. In particular there is rarely diagnostic doubt
about the fantastic and incoherent cases. This contrasts sharply with the
atypical paranoid schizophrenias, where only 47 per cent initially were considered to be schizophrenic psychoses without question. (P $<$ .001).

The coded pre-psychotic personality type is seen in table 34.

Schizoid and self-assertive personalities are most frequent. The subgroups
are small and the variations in personalities great. It is noted that confabulatory paraphrenia rarely have a schizoid personality, which is the most common
type in the other forms of severe deteriorioration.

Table 33

Outcome	Diagnosis of the hospital			
			Reactive psychoses	
	Schizophrenia	Schizophrenia ?	Paranoid	Hysteric
Confabulatory paraphrenia	12	2	0	0
Expansive paraphrenia	20	3	2	1
Fantastic paraphrenia	37	0	1	0
Incoherent paraphrenia	9	1	0	0
Total	78	6	3	1

Table 34

Outcome	Prepsychotic personality							
	Schizoid	Sensitive	Self-assertive	Cycloid	Hysterical	Asocial	Harmonious	Incomplete information
Confabulatory paraphrenia	3	0	3	1	0	3	3	1
Expansive paraphrenia	10	1	6	0	1	4	2	2
Fantastic paraphrenia	11	6	9	0	0	3	5	4
Incoherent paraphrenia	5	0	3	1	0	2	0	1
Total	29	7	19	2	1	12	10	8

The coding of precipitating factors is seen in table 35.

Table 35

Outcome	Precipitating factors						
	Acute mental trauma	Prolonged mental conflicts		Social misery isolation	Somatic disease child-birth	Intoxi-cation mostly alcoholic	No special factors mentione
		Sexual	Others				
Confabulatory paraphrenia	0	0	4	0	3	1	7
Expansive paraphrenia	4	2	2	2	2	0	17
Fantastic paraphrenia	5	7	7	0	2	2	17
Incoherent paraphrenia	0	2	1	1	2	0	6
Total	9	11	14	3	9	3	47

In about one-half of the cases no precipitating factors can be found, which is more frequent than in mild paranoid defects. (P $<$ .01). Expansive cases in particular often have none of the special factors mentioned (65%).

The distribution of affective traits is seen in table 36.

Affective blunting is present from onset in 51 per cent of the patients. As in most other types of paranoid schizophrenia, affective instability which implies impure affect is often found. Severely deteriorated paranoid patients show less depression (P $<$ .001), but more elation, euphoria or exstasy than other paranoid schizophrenics (P $<$ .10). This suggests that elated mood tends to be found already at onset.

Incoherent paraphrenia is an exception, but has the most affective blunting (70%).

The delusional content is seen in Table 37.

Delusions are present, as a rule, from onset. In a few cases delusions emerge for the first time after a long duration of illness, although they are central symptoms in the chronic stages. The typical schizophrenic delusions (Astrup & Noreik, 1966) are more common here than in other types of schizo-

Table 36

Outcome	Affective traits					
	Depression	Elation, euphoria, ecstasy	Perplexity	Anxiety	Affective instability	Emotional blunting
Confabulatory paraphrenia	0	7	0	0	4	6
Expansive paraphrenia	2	12	1	0	8	13
Fantastic paraphrenia	3	16	2	0	14	19
Incoherent paraphrenia	1	0	2	1	4	7
Total	6	35	5	1	30	45

Table 37

Outcome	Delusional content										
	Guilt inferiority	Hypochondria	Ideas of reference	Persecution	Revindication	Megalomania		Fantasy lover	Ideas of high descent	Fantastic ideas of jealousy	No delusions established
						Religious	Other forms				
Confabulatory paraphrenia	1	1	0	6	0	1	5	4	1	1	0
Expansive paraphrenia	1	2	2	14	0	5	12	6	3	0	0
Fantastic paraphrenia	1	4	7	23	1	5	9	1	10	2	2
Incoherent paraphrenia	0	1	3	7	0	2	1	0	0	0	1
Total	3	8	12	50	1	13	27	11	14	3	3

phrenia (P < .001). Thus delusions of a megalomanic character, and ideas of
high descent can give a suspicion that such defects may develop. Incoherent
paraphrenia show less of such delusions, but more persecution (70%).

Types of thought disturbance are seen in Table 38.

Table 38

Outcome	Disturbance of thinking					
	Flight of ideas	Inco- herence	Deper- sona- lisa- tion	Passi- vity	Symbol- ism	No mention of thought disturbance
Confabulatory paraphrenia	0	2	4	6	7	2
Expansive paraphrenia	0	10	10	15	14	0
Fantastic paraphrenia	0	6	20	19	20	4
Incoherent paraphrenia	0	4	6	7	3	0
Total	0	22	40	47	44	6

With regard to thought disturbance, these psychoses differ from the mild
typical paranoid schizophrenias with more incoherence (P < .001) and less
passivity (P < .001). It is noted that only 14% of the confabulatory, but 40% of
the incoherent, have incoherence.

Types of hallucinations are seen in Table 39.

Hallucinations are practically always present from onset. Haptic hallucinations are not especially frequent in fantastic paraphrenia, which in the chronic
stages shows such symptoms.

Age at onset of the psychosis is seen in Table 40.

Incoherent paraphrenia has comparatively low, and fantastic paraphrenia
rather high, age of onset. With regard to age of onset these psychoses do not
differ much from the slightly deteriorated systematic paranoid schizophrenics.
In 33 per cent of the cases the illness starts after 40, as compared with 4% in

Table 39

Outcome	Hallucinations						
	Auditory	Auditory Special forms	Olfactory gustatory	Visual	Haptic		Without hallucination
					Sexual	Others	
Confabulatory paraphrenia	12	0	0	2	3	4	2
Expansive paraphrenia	20	6	0	8	4	6	0
Fantastic paraphrenia	31	6	2	10	6	10	1
Inccherent paraphrenia	10	2	0	2	0	2	0
Total	73	14	2	22	13	22	3

Table 40

Outcome	Age at onset			
	20 years or les	21 - 30 years	31 - 40 years	40 years
Confabulatory paraphrenia	2	5	5	2
Expansive paraphrenia	1	10	6	9
Fantastic paraphrenia	2	9	11	16
Incoherent paraphrenia	0	7	1	2
Total	5	31	23	29

Table 41

	Duration of illness before admission					
Outcome	½ year	½ - 1 year	1 - 2 years	2 - 5 years	5 - 10 years	10 years
Confabulatory paraphrenia	3	1	1	3	2	4
Expansive paraphrenia	6	0	2	8	7	3
Fantastic paraphrenia	8	4	4	9	6	7
Incoherent paraphrenia	2	0	2	5	1	0
Total	19	5	9	25	16	14

severely deteriorated catatonic cases (P $<$ .001), and 2% in severely deteriorated hebephrenic cases (P $<$ .001).

Duration of illness is seen in table 41.

Many cases have quite long duration of illness before admission, and the severe deterioration has developed gradually. Incoherent paraphrenia is an exception. This suggests that the patients often are so disorganized in the beginning of the illness that they cannot manage in the community. Duration of illness tended to be shorter in patients with mild schizophrenic defects.

The types of psychomotor symptoms are seen in Table 42.

It is noted that all but two of the incoherent paraphrenias have psychomotor symptoms, while the majority of the confabulatory cases have no psychomotor symptoms (71%).

The distribution of initial symptoms is seen from Table 43.

Table 42

Outcome	Psychomotor symptoms								
	Inhibition	Blocking	Stupor	Excitation	Mannerism	Agitation Restlessness	Negativism	Varying	No psychomotor disturbances mentioned
Confabulatory paraphrenia	0	0	0	3	0	0	1	1	10
Expansive paraphrenia	0	3	0	9	3	2	2	2	10
Fantastic paraphrenia	0	4	1	7	3	4	2	1	23
Incoherent paraphrenia	0	3	0	4	3	0	2	0	2
Total	0	10	1	23	9	6	7	4	45

Table 43

Outcome	Initial symptoms								
	Transitory periods	Change of personality	Depressive traits	Neurasthenic traits	Ideas of reference suspicious jealous	Impulsive tantrums	Vagrancy, restlessness	Religious or philosophical preoccupation	No special initial symptoms mentioned
Confabulatory paraphrenia	2	8	0	1	6	2	0	0	0
Expansive paraphrenia	1	13	1	3	16	3	0	0	1
Fantastic paraphrenia	7	8	2	3	23	3	3	3	2
Incoherent paraphrenia	0	8	0	1	1	2	0	1	1
Total	10	37	3	8	46	10	3	4	4

Except for incoherent and confabulatory paraphrenia a paranoid onset is most common. Quite a few start with a change of personality. This is seen usually in the incoherent cases (80%), and less in the fantastic cases (21%). A depressive onset is rather rare (3%), but occurs in 14% of the cases with systematic mild paranoid defects.

Table 44 gives the clinical syndrome at onset.

Table 44

Outcome	Clinical syndrome at onset						
	Depression	Excita-tion	Confusion	Paranoid	Hebe-phrenic	Cata-tonic	Hysteri-form
Confabulatory paraphrenia	0	1	0	13	4	1	0
Expansive paraphrenia	0	0	0	26	6	1	0
Fantastic paraphrenia	0	0	0	36	6	5	0
Incoherent paraphrenia	0	0	1	10	5	3	0
Total	0	1	1	85	21	10	0

Compared with the slight paranoid defects hebephrenic and catatonic syndromes are more often noted (P < .001). The incoherent cases in particular have these syndromes. Depression, excitation or confusion are practically absent, but are quite frequent in cases developing slight paranoid defects.

Premorbid intelligence is seen in Table 45.

Quite a few are coded as having below average intelligence (33%). Among the incoherent cases only 50% have average or above average intelligence.

Type of onset of the illness is seen from table 46.

Compared with cases with mild paranoid defects insidious onset is more common (P < .10). Insidious onset is especially characteristic of the incoherent (70%) and expansive (77%) cases.

Body type is coded in Table 47.

Table 45

Outcome	Intelligence		
	Incomplete information	Below average	Average or above
Confabulatory paraphrenia	0	6	8
Expansive paraphrenia	0	7	19
Fantastic paraphrenia	0	12	26
Incoherent paraphrenia	1	4	5
Total	1	29	58

The incoherent cases in particular tend to have a leptosome body build (60%). A pyknic body build is most often found in confabulatory (36%) and fantastic paraphrenia (34%). Among severely deteriorated catatonics and hebephrenics 13 and 9 per cent, respectively, have a pyknic body type.

Observation period since first admission is shown in Table 48.

Compared with the slight paranoid defects, more patients have an observation period of more than 10 years (P < .05). Confabulatory and expansive cases have fewer, with 10 years or longer observation periods, than the fantastic and the incoherent cases (P < .001). Thus we find the longest observation periods among the severely deteriorated subgroups.

Table 46

Outcome	Onset of disease				
	Acute onset without prodromal symptoms	Acute onset after prodromal symptoms	Sub-acute onset	Insidious onset with periodic exacerbations	Insidious onset without oeriodic exacerbations
Confabulatory paraphrenia	0	2	3	7	2
Expansive paraphrenia	2	1	3	7	13
Fantastic paraphrenia	1	6	14	5	12
Incoherent paraphrenia	1	1	1	1	6
Total	4	10	21	20	33

Table 47

Outcome	Body type			
	Incomplete information	Pyknic	Lepto-some	Others or uncharacteristic
Confabulatory paraphrenia	0	5	2	7
Expansive paraphrenia	3	4	8	11
Fantastic paraphrenia	1	13	10	14
Incoherent Paraphrenia	0	1	6	3
Total	4	23	26	35

Table 48

Outcome	Observation period since first admission		
	5 - 9 years	10 - 14 years	15 years or more
Confabulatory paraphrenia	7	4	3
Expansive paraphrenia	16	5	5
Fantastic paraphrenia	10	14	14
Incoherent paraphrenia	1	3	6
Total	34	26	28

f. Discussion

The severe types of paranoid schizophrenic deterioration are quite frequent
in a chronic mental hospital population, but make up a small proportion of
followed-up consecutive first admissions of functional psychoses. They distinguish themselves according to Astrup & Fish (1964) from the mild paranoid defects by being less improved under treatment with psychotropic drugs.

Right from the onset there is rarely any diagnostic doubt about the schizophrenic character of the illness. Premorbid personalities are often schizoid,
and in more than one-half of the cases no precipitating factors can be found.
Depression is rarely seen, while emotional blunting tends to be present from
the onset. Quite a number of cases have hebephrenic or catatonic syndromes

at onset, and change of personality is often an initial symptom. These features indicate that such psychoses at the initial stages have a clear-cut schizophrenic character with poor prognosis.

The severe types of paranoid deterioration have been divided into four subgroups, and several cases represent transitional forms between the groups. At the initial stages there are no marked differences between the four subgroups in the coded clinical characteristics. Confabulatory paraphrenia is an exception to the rule about frequent occurrence of a schizoid personality. Elation, euphoria or ecstasy are often coded. This illustrates that elated mood tends to be present from onset. Here incoherent paraphrenia is an exception. Typical schizophrenic delusions of expansive types are more frequent than in other forms of paranoid schizophrenia in all types except incoherent paraphrenia. The typical schizophrenic thought disturbances are present from onset, but disappear during the chronic stages. Incoherence is rarely seen in confabulatory paraphrenia, but is found in several of the other cases. With progressive course of illness loosening of the associative connections becomes marked in all cases, in particular in the incoherent paraphrenias. Hallucinations are practically always present at admission.

With regard to age of onset, the incoherent paraphrenias start in the youngest, and fantastic paraphrenias in the highest age groups. For the material as a whole, age of onset tends to be later than in severely deteriorated catatonic and hebephrenic schizophrenias, but about as frequent as in the typical paranoid schizophrenias with slight defects. Many cases have a duration of illness of more than five years, though incoherent paraphrenia is an exception. These cases have a more malignant course of illness, and have greater difficulties in achieving social adaptation, so that delayed admission is less possible.

From the coded symptomatology at first admission it does not seem possible to predict what types of severe paranoid defects will develop. The total clinical picture gives better indications, because many cases already at admission show some of the typical symptoms of the defect stages. The course of illness is practically always progressive with the defect symptoms becoming increasingly characteristic. The few cases with incoherent paraphrenia would be difficult to recognize from the beginning. Their initial symp-

toms do not distinguish themselves essentially from other types of schizophrenia, as only one case had a duration of more than five years, and the
severe deterioration was not developed at admission.

Confabulatory, expansive and fantastic paraphrenia have such striking
clinical symptoms, that they are comparatively easy to recognize. There
does not seem to be a development from one type to another, but confabulatory and expansive forms are more limited in their symptomatology, and
tend to show less deterioration than fantastic paraphrenia. It is conceivable
that the more massive symptomatology in the latter type would interfere
more with their ability to adapt.

We have often coded combinations of paranoid, hebephrenic and catatonic
syndromes. The general rule is that cases with initial hebephrenic syndromes develop hebephrenic defects, while those with catatonic syndromes
develop catatonic defects. It is noted that hebephrenic and catatonic syndromes are more common in the severely, than in the mildly deteriorated
paranoid cases (P <. 001). When a severe deterioration develops, high age
of onset and a pyknic body build is more associated with paranoid than catatonic or hebephrenic defects. Incoherent paraphrenia resembles most hebephrenic and catatonic cases at onset, and this is apparently related to the
more severe course of illness.

One might raise the question if psychoses starting out with the characteristics of mild paranoid schizophrenia are transformed into severely deteriorated paranoid cases in the long run.

We noted, in fact, that the observation periods tended to be longer in the
severely than in the mildly deteriorated schizophrenics. Among the slightly
deteriorated paranoid cases we had also shorter duration of illness, and in
particular fewer who had been ill for more than five years prior to admission
(P <.10). This supports an assumption that severe deterioration is associated with a more longstanding illness. In our 1938-50 series 19%, and in our
1951-60 series 11%, of the paranoid defects were classified as severely deteriorated. Thus, severe paranoid deterioration has become more rare in
the recently followed-up cases. No changes have occurred in the classification principles. It is possible that drugs and more effective total push treatment reduce the risk of severe deterioration, although drugs have small
effect on the already established severe paranoid defects. The observation
periods have been shorter in the 1951-60 than in the 1938-50 series. We

have, however, a series of 219 patients re-examined both in 1956 and 1966, with up to 28 years observation periods (Noreik et al., 1967). At both re-examinations the severely deteriorated paranoid cases made up the same proportion of all with paranoid defects. This suggests that one should not expect that with longer observation periods more severe deterioration will be found.

In previous studies (Astrup, 1962; Astrup, Fossum & Holmboe, 1962; Astrup & Noreik, 1966) we noted that close relatives tended to develop similar schizophrenic defects. This tendency was more marked for the slightly than for the severely deteriorated paranoid patients. One might assume that the severe deterioration is less determined by constitutional predisposition than by not yet known environmental factors.

Taking into consideration that severe paranoid defects are rare among consecutive first admissions, one should be careful in predicting such outcomes, even if many prognostically unfavourable items are noted in the clinical picture.

VII. CATATONIC SCHIZOPHRENIA

a. Periodic catatonia

Leonhard points out that periodic catatonia may be difficult to diagnose in the
acute stages. It resembles the cycloid psychoses very much, especially the
motility psychoses of Kleist, which recover without developing schizophrenic
defects (Leonhard, 1966). Periodic catatonia as well as motility psychoses have
a tendency to start with violent psychomotor symptoms, both excitement and
stupor. The motility psychoses present a more pure hyperkinesis or akinesis,
while the periodic catatonias show more of a mixture of excitatory and inhibitory symptoms. In stuporous states there may occur, for instance, steretypes,
grimaces or mannerisms, while the excitatory states can show postural and
facial rigidity.

In periodic catatonia natural grace of movement is absent; reactive and expressive movements lose their meaning. The motility psychoses, on the other
hand, express joy, anger, eroticism in an exaggerated, but natural way. Confusion is also more often present in the motility psychoses.

Periodic catatonia may also resemble the other non-systematic schizophrenias in the acute stages. There are less problems in differentiating them from
affect-laden paraphrenia than from schizophasia. Schizophasia often has marked
psychomotor disturbances at the initial stages, so that it can be difficult to determine whether the symptomatology is predominantly paranoid or catatonic
(Astrup, 1969).

A main characteristic of periodic catatonia is the shifting course of illness
with remissions and exacerbations. We have in our series several patients
who apparently recover from their first catatonic phase, but later develop
schizophrenic defects. As a rule, the defect is slight even after many catatonic exacerbations. In our follow-up material many patients only showed a
psychic lameness, a certain stiffness in the facial expression with inadequate
mimical expressions. Movements are often slow with a tendency to mannerisms.
The patients lack initiative, complain about lack of energy, and have difficul-

ties in achieving contact with other people. Some degree of autism also tends
to be present.

In the slighter defect stages it may be difficult to determine whether the patients acutally show a schizophrenic defect, or some kind of neurotic or psychopathic deviation. In the present series 48 patients were considered to have a
schizophrenic personality changes, while not being chronically psychotic. Se -
veral of these patients correspond to the uncharacteristic residual states which
Huber (1966) calls "reine Defektsyndrome" and often encountered in catamnes-
tic studies.

There is a gradual transition from schizophrenic personality to a chronic
psychotic state in periodic catatonia. The chronic psychotic patients have more
marked psychomotor symptoms, often periodic stupor or excitation. In addition there can be emotional blunting. In the present material there are only a
few cases where impulsive excitements occur so frequently and the patients
are so much out of contact with reality that the deterioration takes on a severe
form.

Phenothiazines were found by Astrup & Fish (1964) to be quite effective in
reducing the symptoms of periodic catatonia. In cases with very long observation periods the schizophrenic defect showed a tendency to fade away and lose
its schizophrenic character. Thus, ten cases classified as having catatonic
defects in 1956 were without such defects in 1966 (Noreik et al. , 1967). The
possibilities of late remissions must therefore be kept in mind in this type of
schizophrenia.

The periodic catatonias are much less in need of prolonged hospital treatment than the systematic catatonias. In the present series 42 cases were
hospitalized at the time of the follow-up. Quite a number of them have later
been discharged. 33 patients were seen in their homes. Among these all but
seven were self-supporting, as a rule on a lower level than before admission.
The remaining 21 cases were in the community, but several of them needed
some type of psychiatric care.

b. Systematic catatonia

Leonhard operates with six types of systematic catatonia. In the present series there were 14 cases of parakinetic, 10 of speech-prompt, 7 of proskinetic, 13 of speech-inactive, 16 of manneristic and 11 of negativistic catatonia.
The total sample of 1938-60 first admissions had 990 cases with schizophrenic

defect, and all six groups make up only seven per cent. The groups are small and comparisons with regard to the coded symptomatology did not reveal any outstanding differences between the subgroups. It was found practical, therefore, to deal with these psychoses as one group compared with the periodic catatonias. In the chronic stages the systematic catatonias reveal marked differences. The following brief summation of the main features will illustrate this.

Parakinetic catatonia is characterized by bizarre actions. Voluntary actions are carried out in an unnatural, awkward way, and the involuntary expressive movements take place jerkily so that they are reminiscent of choreiform movements. These movements appear to be distorted. The patients are frequently grimacing, and speech is "cut up" and expressed as in thrusts.

The most essential symptom of speech-prompt catatonia is talking beside the point. The patients frequently give the correct answer to the simplest indifferent questions. The more difficult and emotionally charged the questions become, the more certainly the patient will disregard the point of the question. In contrast to the readiness of speech, there is a general stiffness of movements. The facial expression is peculiarly empty and expressionless.

The proskinetic catatonics have a tendency to turn towards the examiner and allow themselves to be directed automatically. When spoken to, the patients usually begin to murmur. If it is possible to catch what the patient is saying, the murmuring turns out to be a verbigeration of isolated phrases.

Speech-inactive catatonics give answers very slowly in the earlier stages. In the later stages they do not answer at all. The patients seem to be constantly hallucinating. One can regularly see that they are whispering, sometimes laughing, and at other times looking irritated. From time to time they can be markedly excited. They can only speak to themselves or have pronounced excitements in which they scream and gesticulate towards the empty air.

In manneristic catatonia an increasing impoverishment of involuntary motor activity occurs. This results in a stiffness of posture and movement. In addition there are mannerisms which in the beginning are more prominent than the stiffness. In the later stages the patients have a stiff facial expression and may stay in the same position for hours. During examination opposition can be demonstrated.

Negativistic catatonia is to a great extent a contrast to proskinetic catatonia. They show an active striving against all attempts at making contact. The negativism seems to be of a rather automatic nature. Often an ambi-tendency can be observed. If it is possible to put the patient in a friendly mood, then he may carry out some requests, but only partially. If one tries to overcome the active opposition with force, rather than with friendliness, then a violent negativistic excitement may be released.

A common trait to all systematic catatonias is severe deterioration. Most of the patients need care in all ways with eating, dressing and cleanliness. Verbal communication is poor, and they have practically no working ability.

Phenothiazines (Astrup & Fish, 1964) reduce the incidence of excited and aggressive behaviour in systematic catatonics. Among parakinetic catatonics the parakinesia disappears in some patients, and in negativistic catatonia the positive rejecting behaviour decreases. The severe deterioration persists, and in spite of treatment the patients are usually unable to stay in wards where they are required to care for their own person.

It seems that the phenothiazines make the differential diagnosis between the subgroups of systematic catatonia more difficult. The distinction between non-systematic and systematic catatonia is more reliable. While the periodic catatonias have a shifting course of illness, the systematic catatonias have a more gradually progressive deterioration. The defects are more severe in the systematic catatonias, and as a rule their special features are repeatedly described in the case histories.

In the present series 48 patients were at the time of follow-up treated in mental hospitals, and 17 were under other forms of psychiatric care. Only six lived in their homes, and none of them were able to support themselves. This contrasts very unfavourably with the periodic catatonias.

c. Coded clinical items

Periodic catatonia was found in 49 male and 47 female patients, while 43 men and 28 women had systematic catatonia. Thus, there were slightly more male patients with systematic catatonia.

An initial diagnosis of schizophrenia was given for 73 per cent of the periodic and 93 per cent of the systematic catatonias. Nineteen of the periodic catatonias were originally considered to be reactive psychoses and two manic-depressive. Systematic catatonia is only rarely not recognized as a schizophrenic illness from the beginning.

44 per cent of the periodic catatonias and 54 per cent of the systematic catatonias were coded as having schizoid personality. It is notable that only six per cent of the systematic catatonias were considered to have a sensitive personality,

Table 49

Outcome	Discharge diagnosis of the hospital					
	Schizo-phrenia	Schizo-phrenia ?	Reactive psychoses			Manic depressive
			Depressive	Paranoid	Hysteric and confusional	
Periodic catatonia	73 %	5 %	7 %	3 %	9 %	2 %
Systematic catatonia	93 %	3 %	3 %	0	1 %	0

Table 50

Outcome	Prepsychotic personality								
	Schizoid	Sensi-tive	Self-assertive	Cycloid	Hysteri-cal	Neurotic	Asocial	Harmonious	Incomplete information
Periodic catatonia	44 %	23 %	3 %	1 %	1 %	3 %	5 %	15 %	5 %
Systematic catatonia	54 %	6 %	8 %	0	1 %	1 %	7 %	8 %	14 %

which in our non-schizophrenic psychoses was the most frequent type of personality. For quite a few there is incomplete information. It is likely that what has been coded as premorbid personality may be to a great extent personality changes associated with an insidiously developing systematic catatonia.

40 per cent of the periodic catatonia and 62 per cent of the systematic (P < .01) catatonia showed no precipitating factors. Prolonged mental conflicts (P < .01) and acute mental trauma (P < .05) are more common in periodic catatonia in particular.

Emotional blunting is present from admission in 32 per cent of the periodic

Table 51

Outcome	Affective traits					
	Depression	Elation, euphoria, ecstasy	Perplexity	Anxiety	Affective instability	Emotional blunting
Periodic catatonia	39 %	27 %	35 %	11 %	13 %	32 %
Systematic catatonia	11 %	7 %	24 %	6 %	14 %	72 %

catatonias and in 72 per cent of the systematic catatonias (P < .001). On the other hand, depression, elation, ecstasy, euphoria (P < .001), perplexity (P < .02) and anxiety (P < .001) occur more often in periodic catatonia. These symptoms are prognostically favourable and are seen more often in acute than in insidiously developing schizphrenias.

Table 52

Outcome	Delusional content										
	Guilt inferiority	Hypo-chon-dria	Ideas of refe-rence	Perse-cution	Revin-dica tion	Megalomania		Fanta-sy lover	Ideas of high descent	Fantastic ideas of jealousy	No delu-sions established
						Reli-gious	Other forms				
Periodic catatonia	15 %	8 %	24 %	39 %	1 %	19 %	6 %	6 %	0	2 %	21 %
Systematic catatonia	4 %	11 %	17 %	21 %	0	6 %	0	4 %	3 %	1 %	49 %

Delusions are absent in 21 per cent of the periodic and in 49 per cent of the systematic catatonias (P < .001). Thus, the systematic catatonias are more pure catatonic psychoses on admission, while the periodic catatonias are mostly mixed paranoid-catatonic. Guilt and inferiority, religious and other forms of megalomania are rare in systematic catatonia.

Table 53

Outcome	Disturbance of thinking					
	Flight of ideas	Incoherence	Depersona- lisation	Passivity	Symbolism	No mention of thought disturbance
Periodic catatonia	5 %	38 %	41 %	45 %	17 %	14 %
Systematic catatonia	1 %	38 %	25 %	27 %	10 %	27 %

Thought disturbances are more often absent in the systematic than in the periodic catatonias (P < .05). Typical schizophrenic thought disturbances, such as depersonalization (P < .05), passivity (P < .02), and symbolism are considerably more frequent in periodic catatonia. Such symptoms are usually more characteristic of acutely than of insidiously developing schizophrenias. Incoherence is equally frequent in both groups.

Only 18 per cent showed no hallucinations at admission. Haptic hallucinations were more frequent in periodic (35%) than in systematic catatonia (17%) (P < .01). The same was the case for special forms of auditory hallucinations (17% and 10%). The latter symptoms include hearing of thoughts, conversation with voices, voices with comments on the patient's movements, and voices coming from the patient's own head or body. Thus periodic catatonia shows many of the typical schizophrenic hallucinations.

In all age groups, except 20 years or less, there are more cases of periodic catatonia. 64 per cent of the periodic catatonias had started at age 30 or below, as compared with 76 per cent of the systematic catatonias. Thus, the systematic catatonias tend to start earlier in life.

Less than half a year duration is found for 56 per cent of the periodic catatonias as compared with 17 per cent of the systematic catatonias (P < .001). On the other hand, 7 per cent of the periodic and 37 per cent of the systematic catatonias had lasted more than five years at admission (P < .001). This is probably because the periodic catatonias often start acutely with violent symptoms, so that early hospitalization is needed, while the systematic catatonias develop more insidiously and have at admission already often become chronic.

Table 54

Outcome	Age at onset			
	20 years or less	21 - 30 years	31 - 40 years	40 years
Periodic catatonia	16 %	48 %	30 %	6 %
Systematic catatonia	31 %	45 %	20 %	4 %

Table 55

Outcome	Duration of illness before admission					
	½ year	½ - 1 year	1 - 2 years	2 - 5 years	5 - 10 years	10 years
Periodic catatonia	56 %	13 %	9 %	13 %	6 %	1 %
Systematic catatonia	17 %	4 %	17 %	25 %	14 %	23 %

Table 56

Outcome	Psychomotor symptoms							
	Inhibition	Blocking	Stupor	Excitation	Mannerism	Agitation Restlessness	Negativism	No psycho-motor disturbances mentioned
Periodic catatonia	8 %	39 %	26 %	59 %	17 %	4 %	8 %	0
Systematic catatonia	3 %	35 %	17 %	42 %	31 %	3 %	25 %	7 %

The periodic catatonias have comparatively more inhibition, stupor and excitation (P $<.05$), while the systematic cases have more mannerisms (P $<.05$) and negativism (P $<.01$). This suggests that violent psychomotor symptoms are more frequent in the former, while prognostically unfavourable symptoms are more often found in the latter group. It is remarkable that five systematic cases had no psychomotor symptoms at onset.

Table 57

Outcome	Initial symptoms								
	Transi-tory periods	Change of persona-lity	Depres-sive traits	Neura-sthenic traits	Ideas of reference suspicious jealous	Impul-sive tant-rums	Vag-rancy rest-less-ness	Religi-ous or philo-sophi-cal preoccu-pation	No special initial symptoms mentioned
Periodic catatonia	27 %	33 %	17 %	17 %	25 %	11 %	2 %	4 %	7 %
Systematic catatonia	10 %	68 %	7 %	8 %	24 %	28 %	3 %	4 %	4 %

Transitory periods are quite common in periodic catatonia (P $<.01$). It is mostly difficult to determine whether such periods represent a neurotic or psychotic disturbance. Depressive and neurasthenic traits also often precede the outbreak of the first periodic catatonic phase. In the systematic catatonias change of personality (P < .001), impulsivity and tantrums (P < .01) are more often coded as initial symptoms. These symptoms are prognostically unfavourable and imply as a rule an insidious onset.

Table 58

	Clinical syndrome at onset						
Outcome	Depression	Excitation	Confusion	Paranoid	Hebephrenic	Catatonia	Hysteriform
Periodic catatonia	8 %	9 %	6 %	55 %	11 %	79 %	1 %
Systematic catatonia	3 %	3 %	1 %	37 %	42 %	86 %	0 %

As would be expected, most patients have a catatonic syndrome at onset. In periodic catatonia 20 cases were originally not considered to be catatonic, but rather uncharacteristic depressive, excitatory or confusional states. Quite a number had paranoid syndromes also. The systematic catatonias were often described as hebephrenic syndromes (42%). This suggests that there tends to be an insidious onset, less violent psychomotor symptoms and marked emotional blunting, so that there often are mixed hebephrenic - catatonic syndromes.

It is noted that the systematic catatonic group has 35 per cent with intelligence below average, as compared with only 19 per cent in periodic catatonia (P < .02). Low intelligence is also often coded in severely deteriorated paranoid and hebephrenic cases.

In table 59 the two types of psychoses are quite distinct. Acute onset is found mainly in periodic catatonia (P < .001), while insidious onset without periodic exacerbations is usually coded in systematic catatonia (P < .001).

Both groups are much alike, and very few have a pyknic body type (9%). The leptosome type predominates (46%). The same is true for most other

Table 59

Outcome	Onset of disease				
	Acute onset without prodromal symptoms	Acute onset after prodromal symptoms	Sub- acute onset	Insidious onset with periodic exacerba- tions	Insidious onset withou periodic exacerbations
Periodic catatonia	25 %	36 %	23 %	13 %	3 %
Systematic catatonia	6 %	7 %	32 %	17 %	38 %

schizophrenic subgroups. The only exception was the atypical paranoid schizophrenias with nearly as many having pyknic as leptosome body build. Thus,
the periodic catatonics differ in this respect from the other atypical schizophrenic psychoses.

There are comparatively longer observation periods in the systematic
than in the periodic catatonias. Among the periodic catatonics 46 per cent
have an observation period of less than 10 years, but only 31 per cent of the
systematic catatonias have such a short observation period. Duration of illness before admission tended also to be long in the systematic catatonias.
This suggests that the illness as a rule has to have lasted for a long period
before the typical symptoms of systematic catatonias can be recognized at
follow-up.

d. Discussion

At hospital admission quite a number of differences in symptomatology can be
found between periodic and systematic catatonia. In particular, it is important to be aware that systematic catatonia as a rule is recognized as a schizophrenic illness, while 27 per cent of the periodic catatonias did not receive
a hospital diagnosis of schizophrenia originally.

The periodic catatonias have more admixtures of depression, excitation
and confusion. They are more rich in symptomatology and show in particular more of what we have defined as typical schizophrenic symptoms (Astrup
& Noreik, 1966). For instance, they have more megalomanic delusions
(P < .01), more depersonalization, passivity and symbolism. Haptic hallu-

cinations and special forms of auditory hallucinations are more frequent.
Violent psychomotor symptoms, such as stupor and excitation are also found
more often.

While periodic catatonias often start as mixed paranoid-catatonic states,
the systematic catatonias tend to show more mixed hebephrenic-catatonic
syndromes. Emotional blunting is much more frequent in systematic than
in periodic catatonia, and the same is the case for change of personality as
the initial symptom. This suggests more resemblance to hebephrenic psychoses.

It was noted that cases with less than one year duration of illness were
predominantly periodic catatonias (P < .001). On the other hand, most of
the cases with more than five years duration of illness turned out to be systematic catatonias (P < .001). This suggests that periodic catatonia tends to
develop acutely with violent symptoms, while the systematic catatonics as a
rule start insidiously with less disturbing symptoms and can manage for a
longer period in the community.

Many of the differences between periodic and systematic catatonias are
associated with the insidious onset of the latter group. The systematic catatonics have often been coded as having no factors precipitating the outbreak
of psychosis. It is hard to establish precipitating factors when the psychosis
develops slowly. In the present series the question may also be raised as to
whether what we have coded as external stress has been in most cases adaptation problems due to the illness.

In 68 per cent of the systematic catatonics schizoid personality or incomplete information is coded. Only 6 per cent show sensitive personality, which
is most frequent in functional psychoses with non-schizophrenic outcome.
It is very hard to establish the prepsychotic personality in insidiously developing psychoses. We may often have coded schizoid personality, when there
was a personality change due to the psychosis. The same may be the case
for the frequent coding of below average intelligence.

The systematic catatonias have a comparatively low age of onset, and a
tendency to a long duration. We have defined age of onset as age at the onset
of the psychotic period leading to first admission. This implies that the systematic catatonics not only tend to have been ill for a long time before admission, but also may have shown the first minor symptoms of their illness considerably earlier than coded by us. In periodic catatonia the first symptoms

came as a rule shortly before the actual outbreak of the psychosis.

All this points up the fact that systematic catatonia is even more associated with low age of onset than table 54 suggests. It is probable that the insidious onset at an early age plays a role in the severe deterioration, as severe deterioration is associated with younger age of onset for our total schizophrenic population.

The long duration and observation periods may reflect that considerable time is required to develop the characteristic symptoms of systematic catatonia. One should not exclude the possibility that cases may start out with symptoms suggesting periodic catatonia, which are later transformed into typical systematic catatonia.

Periodic catatonia improves markedly with psychotropic drugs, while systematic catatonia responds very little to drug treatment. This may mean that in periodic catatonia there is still an unstable state with a tendency to remission, while systematic catatonia represents more stable chronic defects. When our 1938-50 and 1951-57 series of first admission were compared, the latter series showed markedly fewer systematic catatonias. Among the 1958-60 admissions there were four systematic and thirteen periodic catatonics. One might suspect that drug treatment and more favourable environmental factors during recent years have counteracted the tendency to develop systematic catatonia. Therefore, we should be careful in predicting an unfavourable outcome with a systematic catatonic defect.

VIII. THE SLIGHTLY DETERIORATED HEBEPHRENIC SCHIZOPHRENIAS

a. Autistic hebephrenia

In the chronic psychotic stages emotional blunting combined with an extreme autism are the central symptoms of autistic hebephrenia. The patients actively shut themselves up, avoid all contacts with others, and tend to reject attempts from others to associate with them. Questions are often not answered, or the patients only say: "I don't know". Autism is a common trait for most schizophrenics, but mainly in the sense of being passively secluded and preoccupied with their own internal experiences. An active seclusion unrelated to delusions, hallucinations or catatonic negativism is rather typical of autistic hebephrenics.

The facial expression of the autistic is stiff and impenetrable, and does not reveal what the patient is feeling. They look morose, and give the impression of being in a state of ill humour. The mood is irritable and dysphoric, and the patients may, if not left in peace, become very aggressive. Aggression does not occur often, but is difficult to predict, because the patients give no warning by verbal utterances, nor by observable behaviour.

The autistics have, as a rule, a good working ability, and in the mental hospital they prefer to work independently, and can often do responsible work. Some work like robots, as if concentration on work is a means of avoiding contact with others. Hallucinations are rarely observed, and the patients do not relate delusions. They may, however, appear paranoid because of their hostile behaviour.

Astrup & Fish (1964) noted that patients who could be persuaded to take phenothiazines became less autistic and more friendly, but the emotional blunting persisted. One patient even took up contact with his family after drug treatment, and went home on leave for the first time in several years.

The autistic hebephrenics have, apart from aggressive episodes, a well-ordered behaviour. This fact, as well as their good working ability, suggests

that the defects are mild. In the present series 12 (34%) were treated in
mental hospitals at the time of follow-up. Ten patients were classified as
"improved with schizophrenic personality changes". These patients had
the characteristic active seclusion, but were too well socially adjusted
to be considered as chronically psychotic.

b. Eccentric hebephrenia

The eccentric hebephrenics have, like the autistics, affective changes in
the direction of irritability, dysphoria, discontent and cheerlessness.
Both types distinguish themselves in this way from the severely deteriorated shallow and silly hebephrenics who are euphoric or show an indifferent contentment with themselves and their surroundings. Although the
eccentric patients may give the impression of being depressed, emotional
blunting is the predominant affective feature. The patients are as a rule
careless with their own personal care, have little interest in their family,
lack initiative and have undergone a reduction in their ethical standards.

The patients often express hypochondriacal sensations, but in a stereotyped way. They are also querulous and repeat the same complaint in a
rather manneristic way. However, the affect is so blunted that the patients
do not give the impression of suffering. It seems more like a habitual man-
nerism of discontent. Just as the patients are stereotyped in their verbal
utterances, they often show eccentric and manneristic behaviour. Many
patients collect worthless things, may carry out compulsive movements,
have rituals of praying, eat only special kinds of food, etc. Some patients
also show antisocial behaviour. In the present series several men have
lived as tramps and beggars and have committed thefts. A few of the women
have been sexually promiscuous.

Phenothiazines make the patients less irritable and counteract the eccentric and manneristic behaviour, but do not essentially affect the emotional
blunting (Astrup & Fish, 1964).

The degree of deterioration is mild in eccentric hebephrenia. In the
mental hospital the patients have, as a rule, a good working ability, can
carry out an adequate conversation and adjust fairly well in open wards.
They are usually quite eager to talk with doctors and others, and distinguish themselves in this way from the autistic hebephrenias.

In the present series 56 patients were classified as improved with schizophrenic personality changes. The distinction between a chronic psychotic state and a minor residual of a schizophrenic psychosis is not clear-cut in eccentric hebephrenia. Emotional blunting is the main psychotic symptom, as delusions are absent and hallucination rarely occur. All cases appear to have some features of emotional blunting, but in the improved ones the social adjustment in the community has been fair, and the general behaviour not so deviant that the patients could be considered as chronically psychotic. The improved cases with eccentric hebephrenia have, as a rule, some lack of initiative, eccentric behaviour and a depressive or dysphoric mood. In some cases the residuals are rather uncharacteristic, with psychic lameness, complaints about lack of energy, irritability and passive seclusion. It may then be difficult to establish whether the patients actually show a schizophrenic defect or some kind of neurotic or psychopathic deviation.

Some patients improve with a prolonged observation period. Thus five cases considered as having schizophrenic defects in 1956, did not show any residual schizophrenic symptoms on re-examination in 1966 (Noreik et al. , 1967). The residuals of periodic catatonia are often rather similar to those of eccentric hebephrenia. In such cases the patients are classified in the catatonic group if the anamnesis shows typical phases of periodic catatonia.

In the present series 26 (22%) only of the eccentric hebephrenics were treated in mental hospitals at the time of the follow-up. Thus the majority can manage with extramural care or live on their own. Altogether 51 patients were personally re-examined in their homes. Forty of them had jobs or managed housework, but the majority had less working capacity than before they became psychotic.

c. Coded clinical items

There were 20 male and 15 female patients with autistic hebephrenia as compared with 88 male and 30 female patients with eccentric hebephrenia. The slight hebephrenic defects thus occur mostly in the male sex, and this is especially the case for eccentric hebephrenia.

Even at first admission no case received the diagnoses of manic-depressive psychoses or reactive hysteric and confusional psychoses. The main differential diagnostic problem has been with reactive depressive psychoses. A diagnosis of schizophrenia is given in 83 per cent for both types. This compares with 69 per cent in our total schizophrenic population.

Schizoid personality is most frequent amounting to 54 per cent in autistic and

Table 60

Outcome	Discharge diagnosis of the hospital			
	Schizophrenia	Schizophrenia ?	Reactive psychoses	
			Depressive	Paranoid
Autistic hebephrenia	83 %	9 %	6 %	3 %
Eccentric hebephrenia	83 %	6 %	9 %	2 %

59 per cent in eccentric hebephrenia. Such personalities made up 38 per cent of our total schizophrenic population. Altogether there are ten alternatives for coding of personality, but none of the other personality types show any essential differences between the two groups of psychoses.

In 57 per cent of the autistic and 53 per cent of the eccentric cases no precipitating factors could be established. Prolonged mental conflicts were coded in 34 per cent of the eccentric and 20 per cent of the autistic cases. Other types of precipitating factors were rare. It is difficult to determine to what extent the external stress may be secondary to the beginning mental disorder.

Table 61

Outcome	Affective traits					
	Depression	Elation, euphoria, ecstasy	Perplexity	Anxiety	Affective instability	Emotional blunting
Autistic hebephrenia	17 %	3 %	20 %	3 %	54 %	69 %
Eccentric hebephrenia	26 %	6 %	20 %	9 %	13 %	80 %

Already at first admission emotional blunting was present in 69 per cent of the autistic and 80 per cent of the eccentric cases. Depression and anxiety are more often coded in the eccentric cases (P < .05), which in the chronic stages tend to have a depressive mood. With regard to the frequent occurrence of affective instability, the autistics resemble the paranoid schizophrenics, but paranoid cases have less emotional blunting.

Table 62

Outcome	Delusional content								
	Guilt inferiority	Hypochondria	Ideas of reference	Perse-cution	Megalomania		Fantasy lover	Fantastic ideas of jealousy	No delusions established
					Reli-gious	Other forms			
Autistic hebephrenia	3 %	17 %	23 %	60 %	9 %	0 %	9 %	3 %	20 %
Eccentric hebephrenia	3 %	20 %	31 %	46 %	9 %	3 %	4 %	0 %	25 %

In 25 per cent of the eccentric and 20 per cent of the autistic cases no delusions could be established. Persecutory delusions were found in 60 per cent of the autistic and 46 per cent of the eccentric patients. Combining the items of hypochondria and ideas of reference, these are slightly more common in eccentric hebephrenia. Although delusions are absent in the chronic stages, the eccentric cases have a tendency to hypochondriacal and complaining behaviour, while the autistics are more hostile towards the environment. The differences are too small to have predictive value.

It is noted that absence of thought disturbance, incoherence and depersonalization are more often coded in the eccentric cases. The autistics have comparatively more symbolism and resemble in this way the paranoid schizophrenics.

Although hallucinations tend to be absent in the chronic stages, only 31 per cent of the autistic and 21 per cent of the eccentric cases are without hallucinations on admission. Visual hallucinations were coded in 13 eccentric, and in one of the autistic cases. Other types of hallucinations showed essentially no differences.

Table 63

Outcome	Disturbance of thinking				
	Incoherence	Depersonalisation	Passivity	Symbolism	No mention of thought disturbance
Autistic hebephrenia	9 %	31 %	43 %	34 %	14 %
Eccentric hebephrenia	19 %	42 %	41 %	23 %	25 %

Table 64

Outcome	Age at onset				
	20 years or less	21 - 30 years	31 - 40 years	40 years	
Autistic hebephrenia	11 %	34 %	34 %	20 %	
Eccentric hebephrenia	16 %	56 %	22 %	5 %	

Among autistic hebephrenics the psychosis tended to start later in life. Thus 54 per cent began after 30 years of age as compared with 27 per cent in eccentric hebephrenia (P < .01). With regard to higher age of onset the autistics resemble more the paranoid schizophrenics. Eccentric hebephrenia starts earlier in life than most other types of schizophrenia (56% above 30 years in the total schizophrenic population). (P < .001.)

Very few autistic cases have a duration of less than half a year prior to ad-

Table 65

	Duration of illness before admission					
Outcome	½ year	½ - 1 year	1 - 2 years	2 - 5 years	5 - 10 years	10 years
Autistic hebephrenia	11 %	3 %	17 %	20 %	26 %	23 %
Eccentric hebephrenia	23 %	7 %	20 %	·27 %	16 %	7 %

sion. Altogether 49 per cent of the autistics have been sick for more than five years as compared with 23 per cent of the eccentric cases (P < .02). Eccentric hebephrenia comes closer to the average for our total schizophrenic population (27% less than half a year, and 26% more than 5 years).

Table 66

	Psychomotor symptoms								
Outcome	Inhibition	Blocking	Stupor	Excitation	Manner-ism	Agitation Restless-ness	Negati-vism	Varying	No psychomotor disturbances mentioned
Autistic hebephrenia	3 %	14 %	6 %	9 %	17 %	11 %	11 %	3 %	37 %
Eccentric hebephrenia	14 %	31 %	5 %	15 %	20 %	5 %	6 %	3 %	33 %

In the majority of the patients with slight hebephrenic defects psychomotor symptoms have been present. Inhibition and blocking are more frequent in eccentric than in autistic hebephrenia (P $<$ .05). Mannerisms are found with about the same frequency in the two groups, although later the eccentrics develop manneristic and stereotyped behaviour.

Table 67

Outcome	Initial symptoms								
	Transitory periods	Change of personality	Depressive traits	Neurasthenic traits	Ideas of reference suspicious jealous	Impulsive tantrum	Vagrancy restlessness	Religious or philosophical preoccupation	No special initial symptoms mentioned
Autistic hebephrenia	9 %	54 %	9 %	6 %	40 %	14 %	9 %	3 %	-
Eccentric hebephrenia	14 %	59 %	13 %	11 %	28 %	16 %	8 %	9 %	-

The most frequent initial symptom is change of personality, but this symptom occurs less often in our total schizophrenic population (35%) (P $<$. 001). The autistics start more often with paranoid symptoms, such as ideas of reference, suspiciousness and jealousy. Transitory periods, depressive and neurasthenic traits, religious and philosophical preoccupations are slightly more common in eccentric hebephrenia.

Table 68

Outcome	Clinical syndrome at onset					
	Depression	Confusion	Paranoid	Hebephrenic	Catatonic	Hysteriform
Autistic hebephrenia	6 %	0 %	77 %	60 %	6 %	0 %
Eccentric hebephrenia	12 %	1 %	63 %	77 %	9 %	2 %

In our total schizophrenic population 291 cases were coded as having a hebephrenic syndrome initially. Among these 64 per cent developed hebephrenic defects. An initial hebephrenic syndrome was coded in 90 per cent of the patients
with severe hebephrenic deterioration (82 cases), 11 per cent of the paranoid
defects (588 cases), and 25 per cent of the catatonic defects (167 cases). Although there is a clear association between an initial hebephrenic syndrome
and hebephrenic outcome, the predictive value of this syndrome is limited.
We note that the autistics have more paranoid and less hebephrenic symptoms
than the eccentrics. Depression and catatonic symptoms are mainly found in
eccentric hebephrenica.

We had coded 14 per cent of the autistics and 20 per cent of the eccentrics
as below average intelligence. The illness starts at a younger age in the eccentrics, and the prodromal of the illness may give a false impression of low
premorbid intelligence.

An insidious onset was found in 72 per cent of the autistic and in 62 per cent
of the eccentric cases. This compares with 51 per cent in our total schizophrenic population. Insidious onset was also frequent in the severely deteriorated hebephrenics (68%).

Pyknic body type was coded in 20 per cent of the autistic and in 9 per cent
of the eccentric cases, while 43 and 52 per cent, respectively, had leptosome
body build. Here the autistics resemble the paranoid schizophrenics.

Since first admission 49 per cent of the eccentrics and 34 per cent of the
autistics had an observation period of less than 10 years. Duration of illness
also tended to be shorter in the eccentric cases. This may mean that the
typical symptom complex of autistic hebephrenia needs a longer time to develop.

d. Discussion

Fish & Astrup (1964) re-classified hospitalized chronic schizophrenics after
four to seven years. In eccentric as well as autistic hebephrenia the classification was changed in few cases. This suggests that the two types of slight
hebephrenic deterioration can be fairly well distinguished from each other
and are quite stable clinical states over many years. However, we must make
the reservation that schizophrenic residuals tend to fade away over very prolonged observation periods. In eccentric hebephrenia several cases show such
small personality deviations that there may even be doubt about the schizo-

phrenic outcome of the illness. Furthermore, the follow-up shows that the majority of the patients are able to live in the community. The social adaptation may be fairly good in spite of the hebephrenic defects.

In a previous study of chronic schizophrenics in Gaustad Hospital there were nearly as many autistic as eccentric hebephrenics (Astrup, 1962). The present study shows that eccentric hebephrenia is much more frequent among consecutive first admissions. But 10 of 23 cases re-examined in Gaustad Hospital were autistics. This suggests that these patients, because of hostile behaviour are less likely to leave the hospital, and therefore accumulate disproportionally among the chronically hospitalized. It seems also that a longer time is needed to develop the typical autistic defects. Furthermore, we have to consider that the autistic symptomatology is counteracted by the phenothiazines. Therefore, autistic defects may have become more difficult to recognize. In our series of 1938-50 admissions the autistics made up 33 per cent of all those with slight hebephrenic defects (Astrup, Fossum & Holmboe, 1962), as compared with 23 per cent in the total 1938-60 series. This suggests that autistic hebephrenia has become more rare during later years. Our 1958-61 admissions showed less schizophrenic deterioration and more personality changes than our previous series (Holmboe et al. , 1968). The personality changes become more and more the types seen in eccentric hebephrenia. In the present series the severely deteriorated hebephrenics made up 35 per cent of all hebephrenic defects and were most common among the 1938-50 admissions. It seems that more active somatic, psychological and social treatment may change the hebephrenic outcome in the direction of milder defects of the eccentric type.

A comparison of coded clinical characteristics at the time of hospital admission does not reveal marked differences between the two types of slight hebephrenic deterioration. This implies that it is difficult to predict what form may develop in the chronic stages.

The typical autistic symptoms need more time to develop, as duration of illness and observation periods tend to be longer. These patients also become psychotic later in life. In several ways they resemble more the groups which develop paranoid defects. The initial symptoms are quite often paranoid with ideas of reference, suspiciousness and jealousy. On admission the majority have paranoid syndromes. Persecutory ideas were frequent, and all but seven cases had some kind of delusions. Thought disturbances often included

symbolism such as in the delusional interpretations of the paranoid schizophrenics. Quite a number also had affective instability, outburst of rage,
irritability, and sudden unmotivated mood-swings from one day to another.
These emotional disturbances cannot be coded as affective blunting. But
they have the character of inappropriate affect and occur predominantly in
the paranoid cases.

Eccentric hebephrenia starts more often with change of character, transitory periods of nervousness, neurasthenic and depressive traits. The coded
items suggest a greater tendency to depression, psychomotor inhibition and
blocking. Pyknic body type is rare, and the great majority of the patients
are men.

For both forms of slight hebephrenic deterioration there are smaller differential diagnostic problems than in most other subgroups with schizophrenic course of illness. Thus the initial diagnosis was in 90 per cent
schizophrenia.

The hebephrenic nature of the illness can usually be traced back to the
initial stages. In most cases a hebephrenic syndrome has been coded. When
this syndrome is present, the most likely outcome is a hebephrenic defect.
Paranoid symptoms are frequent, while catatonic traits are rare. Note that
paranoid and catatonic symptoms only occur during short time periods.

Several other factors are associated with the hebephrenic outcome. Onset
tends to be insidious with a change of personality as the initial symptom.
Emotional blunting is present as a rule on admission. The frequent coding
of schizoid personality may represent the effect of an insidiously developing
hebephrenic illness, more than true premorbid traits. Earlier onset and
lack of precipitating factors also increase the probability of hebephrenic
outcome.

The symptom coding gives rather crude quantitative measures of the clinical state at admssion. No single factor has a great predictive value. An
evaluation of the total clinical picture with emphasis on the symptom constellations seems most useful for picking out cases with a great risk of a
hebephrenic course of illness.

IX. THE SEVERELY DETERIORATED HEBEPHRENIC SCHIZOPHRENIAS

a. Shallow hebephrenia

In the chronic stage these psychoses show a marked flattening of affect. The mood is usually cheerful or contented, but periodically the patients may be hallucinated, irritable, aggressive and excited.

During the excited periods the patients hear voices, but may in addition have hallucinations in other sensory fields. Usually the patients realize the morbid nature of the hallucinations, when the excitatory periods are over.

The shallow hebephrenics are normally able to carry on a simple conversation, but are far less adequate than the slightly deteriorated hebephrenics. In particular, they give no emotional response, when topics which should affect them are discussed. These patients have a general lack of initiative and small working interest or ability. As a rule they are able to look after themselves. In the present series 42 patients were treated in mental hospitals at the time of re-examination. Their periods of aggressiveness were the main reason for hospitalization. Otherwise, more would have managed with out-patient care.

In experimental studies such patients show severe disturbances of higher nervous activity. In particular, they had many signs of dissociation in verbal and motor tasks (Astrup, 1962). Psychotropic drugs (Astrup & Fish, 1964) reduce the hallucinatory excitements, but affect the emotional flattening very little.

b. Silly hebephrenia

The silly or "läppische" hebephrenics show a circumscribed defect state; the description of this by Kraepelin (1910) has been taken over practically unchanged by Leonhard (1966).

An intensive affective blunting is associated with a mood which varies from being contented to being mildly cheerful. A smiling or a pronounced giggling is particularly characteristic, and this becomes prominent under the influence of every external stimulus. In particular they tend to giggle when spoken to. This does not occur in the shallow hebephrenics. The silly hebephrenics tend to play childish tricks on other patients and nurses, and may sometimes even be malicious. In the chronic stages they do not, as a rule, hallucinate, and they do not have periodic excitements like the shallow hebephrenics.

The silly hebephrenics have little or no initiative and practically no working ability. They are so disorganized that they cannot carry on an ordered conversation, but answer simple questions adequately. In the present series 15 patients were treated in mental hospitals at the time of the follow-up. These patients were rarely aggressive and could care for their own person with some supervision. It was therefore possible for many patients to manage with out-patient psychiatric care. However, they were more deteriorated than the shallow hebephrenics.

In experimental studies they showed more signs of disturbances of higher nervous activity than the shallow hebephrenics. The greater emotional lability appeared to be related to more signs of dissocation of autonomic responses (Astrup, 1962).

The phenothiazines have no effect on the emotional blunting, but the patients become calmer, play less tricks and appear less disturbed and excited. The smiling and giggling persist. (Astrup & Fish, 1964.)

c. Coded clinical items

There were 35 male and 19 female patients with shallow hebephrenia. Eleven male and 17 female patients had silly hebephrenia. Thus there is a reverse sex distribution in the two forms of severe hebephrenic deterioration (P < .05).

In both types of psychoses there were rarely diagnostic doubts at first admission. Altogether 92 per cent received a diagnosis of schizophrenia, four per cent schizophrenia (?) and the remaining reactive psychoses. A diagnosis of schizophrenia was given in 83 per cent of the slightly deteriorated hebephrenias and in 69 per cent of the total schizophrenic population.

Schizoid personality is most frequent, amounting to 72 per cent in shallow, and 54 per cent in silly hebephrenics. Fifty-eight per cent of slight hebephrenic defects, and 38 per cent of the total schizophrenic population had this personality type. It is very probable that what is conceived of as premorbid schizoid personality, often may be character traits due to the beginning schizophrenic illness. The shallow cases have very little emotional contact with other people and great lack of initiative. This appears to be a direct continuation of schizoid behaviour for many years before the illness is recognized. Possibly the marked affective flattening is a kind of defence against the stresses of interpersonal relationships.

Absence of precipitating factors was coded in 45 per cent of the total schizophrenic population, and in 54 per cent of the slightly deteriorated hebephrenics. We have 63 per cent in shallow and 75 per cent in silly hebephrenia. It is difficult to determine to what extent the precipitating factors are accidental events or play an essential role in eliciting the psychotic breakdown. Only two cases had been exposed to acute mental trauma, and in seven cases the illness started in connection with somatic disease or childbirth. Prolonged mental conflicts were most frequent, and may have been consequences of adaptation problems due to the illness.

Table 69

Outcome	Affective traits					
	Depression	Elation, euphoria, ecstasy	Perplexity	Anxiety	Affective instability	Emotional blunting
Shallow hebephrenia	6	5	8	2	8	48
Silly hebephrenia	3	2	7	1	2	25
Total	9	7	15	3	10	73

For each patient one or two predominant affective traits were coded. Compared with the total schizophrenic population, emotional blunting is much more common in the severely deteriorated hebephrenics (P < .001). This symptom is found in 54 per cent of the slightly deteriorated hebephrenics. Emotional blunting is a very unfavourable symptom, indicating that at admission these psychoses are already hard-core groups. The rare occurrence of prognostically favourable symptoms, such as depression, elation, euphoria and ecstasy is noted.

Table 70

Outcome	Delusional content										
						Megalomania				Fantastic ideas of jealousy	No delusions established
	Guilt inferiority	Hypochondria	Ideas of reference	Persecution	Revindication	Religious	Other forms	Fantasy lover	Ideas of high descent		
Shallow hebephrenia	1	3	7	21	1	1	5	2	2	1	25
Silly hebephrenia	0	3	8	14	0	1	2	0	0	0	7
Total	1	6	15	35	1	2	7	2	2	1	32

The majority of the severely deteriorated hebephrenics have delusions initially, which disappear in the chronic stages. Absence of delusions is associated more with shallow than with silly hebephrenia. In silly hebephrenia ideas of reference and persecution are about as common as in the total schizophrenic population (P < .10).

The two subgroups do not essentially distinguish themselves from each other. Incoherence, depersonalization and passivity are about as frequent as in other types of schizophrenia. Symbolism is, however, rarely seen in the severely deteriorated hebephrenics. This symptom is more frequent in the mildly deteriorated hebephrenics (25 per cent) (P < .10).

Table 71

Outcome	Disturbance of thinking					
	Flight of ideas	Incoherence	Depersonalisation	Passivity	Symbolism	No mention of thought disturbance
Shallow hebephrenia	0	12	23	32	9	11
Silly hebephrenia	0	7	13	14	4	7
Total	0	19	36	46	13	18

Table 72

Outcome	Hallucinations						
	Auditory	Auditory Special forms	Olfactory gustatory	Visual	Haptic		Without hallucination
					Sexual	Others	
Shallow hebephrenia	38	14	2	11	3	9	8
Silly hebephrenia	18	6	2	5	3	3	7
Total	56	20	4	16	6	12	15

At onset both types of hebephrenic psychoses have a distribution of hallucinations which lies close to that of our total schizophrenic population. Absence of hallucination is noted in 15 per cent of the shallow and 25 per cent of the silly hebephrenias. The symptom coding gives no special indications that all kinds of hallucinations tend to disappear in silly hebephrenia, while auditory hallucinations are a characteristic feature of shallow hebephrenia in the chronic stages.

In 88 per cent of the severely deteriorated hebephrenics the illness started before the age of 30. This compares with 44 per cent in the total schizophrenic population (P $<$ .001) and 66 per cent in the slightly deteriorated hebephrenics (P $<$ .001).

Among all hebephrenic defects, the severely deteriorated made up 54 per cent of those with age of onset of 20 years or below, 24 per cent of those between 20 and 30 years, and 16 per cent above 30 years. Thus the risk of severe hebephrenic deterioration is clearly associated with young age of onset. No difference could be established between silly and shallow hebephrenia. 68 and 67 per cent respectively develop their first psychotic symptoms after the age of 20 when slight defects are most common.

In the total schizophrenic population 27 per cent and among slightly deteriorated hebephrenics 20 per cent had a duration of illness of less than half a year. The corresponding figure for the shallow and silly hebephrenics is 15 per cent. Only four cases had an acute onset in addition. We have defined duration as the period the patient has been continually psychotic before hospital admission. As the onset tends to be insidious, prodromals before the actual appearance of psychotic symptoms are, as a rule, found for a considerable period. Thus, a severe hebephrenic deterioration is mainly found in patients who have been sick for a long period before hospital admission.

Mannerisms are markedly more frequent in the shallow (32 per cent) than in the silly hebephrenias (18 per cent) (n.s.). This symptom is prognostically unfavourable and occurs in 19 per cent with slight hebephrenic defects, and 13 per cent of the total schizophrenic population.

It is noted that excitation occurs in 28 per cent of the severely and 14 per cent of the slightly deteriorated hebephrenics (P<.10). This can be related to the more excited behaviour of the former in the chronic stages.

Table 73

Outcome	Initial symptoms								
	Transitory periods	Change of personality	Depressive traits	Neurasthenic traits	Ideas of reference suspicious jealous	Impulsive tantrums	Vagrancy restlessness	Religious or philosophical preoccupation	No spec init symptoms mentioned
Shallow hebephrenia	2	42	7	2	11	19	5	2	1
Silly hebephrenia	1	21	1	7	6	9	1	0	1
Total	3	63	8	9	17	28	6	2	2

Both silly and shallow hebephrenia start predominantly with prognostically unfavourable symptoms, such as change of personality, impulsivity and tantrums. These symptoms imply, as a rule, a longstanding illness, and occur less often in the total schizophrenic population (P<.001 & P<.001). Among slightly deteriorated hebephrenics 58 per cent had a change of personality and 16 per cent impulsivity or tantrums.

Table 74

	Clinical syndrome at onset						
Outcome	Depression	Excita-tion	Confusion	Paranoid	Hebe-phrenic	Cata-tonic	Hysteri-form
Shallow hebephrenia	1	0	1	34	50	5	1
Silly hebephrenia	0	1	1	16	24	2	0
Total	1	1	2	50	74	7	1

At onset silly and shallow hebephrenias have a rather similar distribution of
symptoms. As should be expected, hebephrenic syndromes are markedly more
frequent than in the total schizophrenic population. Among the slightly deteriorated hebephrenics a hebephrenic syndrome was coded in 73 per cent of the cases.
They have more depressive (11 per cent) (P $<$ .01) and paranoid symptoms (66
per cent). Hebephrenic syndromes were coded in 11 per cent of patients with
paranoid defects and 25 per cent of patients with catatonic defects. This implies
that if a hebephrenic syndrome is present at onset, the most likely outcome is
a hebephrenic defect. In the total schizophrenic population 64 per cent of the
cases with hebephrenic syndromes at onset developed hebephrenic defects.

We have coded below-average intelligence in 30 per cent of the shallow and
36 per cent of the silly hebephrenias. In slightly deteriorated hebephrenics
there are 19 per cent. For all severely deteriorated patients a large proportion
have low intelligence. There are two possibilities which may explain the findings.
The first is that many patients have developed the illness insidiously, so that
what is conceived of as low premorbid intelligence reflects to a great extent the
beginning symptoms of the illness. The other is that low intelligence favours
the development of a severe defect. In the present series 73 per cent of the
cases with below average intelligence had an insidious onset as compared with
66 per cent of the remaining cases. Thus, there is only a slight difference in
favour of the first hypothesis.

It is noted that 67 per cent of the shallow and 71 per cent of the silly hebephrenics had an insidious onset of illness. This compares with 51 per cent in the total schizophrenic population and 64 per cent in the slightly deteriorated hebephrenics. Only 5 of the severely deteriorated hebephrenics had an acute onset without prodromal symptoms. Accordingly, these psychoses have nearly always presented some kind of symptom for a long time before the psychotic breakdown occurs.

A leptosome body build was found in 41 per cent of the shallow and 61 per cent of the silly hebephrenics. This body type was coded in 39 per cent of the total schizophrenic population and in 50 per cent of the slight hebephrenic defects. For pyknic body type the percentages are respectively 7, 11, 19 and 11. The rare occurrence of a pyknic body type is thus common to all the hebephrenic psychoses.

Altogether 54 per cent had an observation period of more than 10 years, which is the same as in the slightly deteriorated hebephrenics. Thus, the severe hebephrenic deterioration is not related to the length of the observation period. In our total schizophrenic population 53 per cent had more than 10 years observation period. For the silly hebephrenics it was noted that 57 per cent came into this category. There is thus only a slight tendency for these cases to require more time to be recognized.

d. Discussion

At the chronic stages shallow and silly hebephrenia are as a rule not difficult to differentiate from each other. However, the coded clinical characteristics at onset give few indications about what type of defect is likely to occur. The total clinical picture may give more information, because at admission several cases already show the characteristic symptoms of the defect stages. This is mainly the case when the patients have had a long duration of illness before admission.

Fish & Astrup (1964) reclassified schizophrenics after up to a four year period. Among 19 cases with silly hebephrenia, all remained in the same category. Only nine of 14 shallow hebephrenics received the same classification. Four cases were transferred from other subgroups to this group. Thus the latter psychoses appear to be more variable in symptomatology over the years and have less specific symptoms.

The next problem is to what extent the characteristics at admission may indicate the development of a severe hebephrenic deterioration. None of the coded items are specifically associated with these types of psychoses. They show nevertheless certain features more often than in other types of schizophrenia. Premorbid personalities are as a rule schizoid, though often what is coded as a schizoid personality may be more a sign of an insidiously developing hebephrenia than the actual premorbid personality. Precipitating factors are as a rule absent or doubtful. Emotional blunting tends to be present already at admission, and depressive features are rare. Age of onset is comparatively low. As a rule the patients have been sick for a long time before hospital admission. The initial symptoms are very often change of character, impulsivity or tantrums. An acute onset is rare, most cases have an insidious onset.

Already at first admission there is rarely any doubt about the schizophrenic nature of the illness. A major reason for this is the tendency for the patient to show signs of illness for a long time before hospitalization. Furthermore, a variety of prognostically unfavourable factors, associated with a schizophrenic course of illness are frequent. As a rule the hebephrenic traits can be traced back to the initial stage. When several syndromes occur in combination the most likely outcome is a hebephrenic defect.

At follow-up the main problem is to differentiate it from slight hebephrenic defects, which also are characterized by an affective blunting. In these defects the affect has in addition a depressive, irritable, or morose character, while the affect is more euphoric or cheerful in the severe hebephrenic defects. The behaviour is also more disorganized in the latter.

On the basis of the total clinical picture, it is a rule not difficult to distinguish between severe and slight hebephrenic deterioration.

The coded symptomatology at hospital admission is rather similar in the severely and the slightly deteriorated hebephrenics. Considering that slight hebephrenic deterioration is about twice as common as severe hebephrenic deterioration, one should be careful in predicting the latter outcome.

Among 1938-57 admissions the severely deteriorated hebephrenics made up 9.3 per cent of all schizophrenic defects as compared with only 2.2 per cent of the 1958-60 admissions. The most likely explanation of this difference is more effective treatment during the last period.

For all first admissions to Gaustad Hospital during the years 1938-50 43 per cent developed schizophrenic deterioration and 12 per cent minor

schizophrenic residual symptoms. For 1958-61 admissions there were respectively 24 per cent and 21 per cent (Holmboe et al., 1968). This might support an assumption that psychotropic drugs and other therapeutic activities
become increasingly effective in preventing deterioration.

The present study suggests that the frequency of severe hebephrenic deterioration is not related to the length of the observation period. A series
of 219 patients were followed up in 1956 and re-examined in 1966 (Noreik et al.,
1967). The number of severely deteriorated hebephrenics decreased from 8 to
6, and the mildly deteriorated hebephrenics from 17 to 12. All types of severely deteriorated schizophrenics decreased from 32 to 22. Accordingly, a very
prolonged observation period (up to 28 years) has lead to less hebephrenic outcome and less severe deterioration. The criteria for classification have not
changed, so that other factors must explain the findings.

Previous studies by Astrup and Fish (1964) showed rather small effects of
drugs on chronic cases with severe hebephrenic deterioration. The experiences of the prolonged follow-up (Noreik et al., 1967) cast some doubt upon
the assumption of the irreversibility of severe hebephrenic deterioration. Increased age, treatment or spontaneous changes over a long time may modify
the clinical picture. The main effect of modern somatic and environmental
treatment is probably to prevent the development of severe hebephrenic deterioration.

Close relatives of patients with severe hebephrenic deterioration rarely
develop identical clinical pictures (Astrup, Fossum & Holmboe, 1962; Astrup
& Noreik, 1966). Thus neither genetic background, nor individual clinical
symptoms at the initial stage contribute essentially to the prediction of outcome. Shallow and silly hebephrenia may, as Leonhard argues, represent
alterations of certain functional systems. The present study cannot determine the roles of psychodynamic or physiological factors in the mechanisms
of the deterioration. But the rare occurrence among 1958-60 admissions suggests that environmental factors during the coming years can prevent the development of severe hebephrenic deterioration.

X. SUMMARY

I. The general background of the follow-up series from Gaustad Hospital is presented.

II. The chapter deals with the author's own experience with the Kleist-Leonhard classifications in schizophrenia. Furthermore, the following is discussed: the history of the classificatory system, decision rules for differentiating between the 19 subgroups, genetic and neurophysiological aspects, long-term changes of the clinical picture, problems of drug treatment and psychosocial treatment. A fundamental subdivision is shown between systematic and non-systematic schizophrenias.

III. The chapter describes the general characteristics of a material of 990 chronic schizophrenics admitted to Gaustad Hospital during the years 1938-60. These have all been followed up with an observation period ranging between 5 and 34 years. The majority of the patients have been personally re-examined by a team of psychiatrists.

IV. 349 cases were classified as atypical paranoid schizophrenias. They were subdivided into 230 cases of affect-laden paraphrenia and 119 cases of schizophasia. The main common trait of these psychoses was a tendency to remitting course of illness and rather slight defects in the chronic stages.

An analysis of the clinical characteristics at the onset of the illness revealed that both types of psychoses had massive schizophrenic symptomatology in the initial stages. Schizophasia did not show marked differences from our total population with schizophrenic defects, but some features could be related to their atypical course of illness.

Affect-laden paraphrenia could be distinguished in several ways from the other types of schizophrenia. This type of psychosis occurred predominantly in the female sex, tended to start late in life and showed marked affective traits at the onset, in particular depression. Differential diagnosis is difficult

towards reactive psychoses, especially of a paranoid type. Even after prolonged follow-up there may often be doubt as to whether these psychoses shall
be classified as schizophrenic or non-schizophrenic states. The awareness of
the characteristics of this group is practically important because such psychoses occur frequently.

V.   151 cases had chronic hallucinatory psychoses. These could be subdivided into 90 cases of phonemic and 61 cases of hypochondriacal paraphrenia.
At follow-up these psychoses could be fairly well separated from each other.

From the analysis of the coded symptomatology at onset, the two groups
showed some differences in that from the beginning hypochondriacal paraphrenia
had more clear-cut characteristics of paranoid schizophrenia. It also seemed
that these psychoses needed more time to develop the typical defect stage. Haptic
hallucinations were more frequent at the initial stage of hypochondriacal paraphrenia, but often developed over the years. On the other hand, several cases
with phonemic paraphrenia in the beginning had haptic hallucinations which later
disappeared.

Both types of psychoses were characterized from the beginning by massive
schizophrenic thought disturbances, such as depersonalization, passivity and
symbolism. Persecutory delusions and sensitive delusions of reference were
frequent at onset, but disappeared later. Practically all cases started with hallucinations as key symptoms. In particular these cases presented from the beginning auditory hallucinations which represented their main common feature.

VI.   88 cases with schizophrenic outcome were classified as severely deteriorated paranoid schizophrenias. These cases were, according to the symptomatology and follow-up, subdivided into confabulatory, expansive, fantastic and
incoherent types.

At hospital admission there is rarely doubt about the schizophrenic character of the illness. Prognostically unfavourable items are frequently seen at onset. Premorbid personalities tend to be schizoid, change of character is often
an initial symptom, and precipitating factors are lacking in most cases. Depression is rarely seen, while emotional blunting, as a rule, is present on admission. A number of cases have hebephrenic or catatonic syndromes at onset,
while this is rarely the case in psychoses with slight paranoid deterioration.

The four types of defects can be distinguished from each other fairly well at
follow-up. From the coded symptomatology at first admission, it does not seem

possible to predict what types of defects will develop. The total clinical picture gives better indications, because at admission many cases already show some of the characteristic symptoms of the defect stages. During the later years these psychoses have become rare, and it is probable that drugs and other environmental factors are counteracting the tendency to develop severe paranoid deterioratinn.

VII.   167 cases with schizophrenic outcome were classified as having catatonic defects. The patients were subclassified into 96 periodic catatonics and 71 systematic catatonics. The periodic catatonics present mainly personality changes or slight deterioration, while the systematic catatonics are severely deteriorated.

At hospital admission periodic catatonia has more violent psychomotor symptoms, starts often as mixed paranoid-catatonic states, while the systematic catatonias present more mixed hebephrenic-catatonic syndromes.

The periodic catatonias have a more acute onset and shorter duration of illness prior to admission. They also tend to start later in life.

The general rule is that prognostically unfavourable individual symptoms are more frequent in systematic catatonia. Many of these symptoms are apparently associated with an insidious psychotic development.

However, there is the possibility that systematic catatonia may run an unfavourable course in cases which initially had prospects of a favourable outcome. In the present series it is noted that systematic catatonia has become rarer with the introduction of drug treatment and better environmental conditions during recent years. If this trend continues, systematic catatonias may become rare forms of the catatonic psychoses.

VIII.   153 cases with schizophrenic outcome were classified as slightly deteriorated hebephrenics. These cases were subdivided into 35 autistic and 118 eccentric hebephrenias.

The two types of slight hebephrenic deterioration can be fairly well distinguished from each other in the chronic stages. A comparison of coded clinical characteristics at the time of hospital admission reveals some differences between the two types of hebephrenic psychoses. Thus the autistic cases tend to become ill later in life, have more paranoid features, and need as a rule a longer time to develop the characteristic defect symptoms.

Already at first admission the schizophrenic character of the illness is normally established. The hebephrenic traits can usually be traced back to the initial stages. It seems that modern treatment changes the hebephrenic outcome in the direction of milder defects of the eccentric type.

IX. 82 cases with schizophrenic outcome were classified as severely deteriorated hebephrenics. These cases were subdivided into 54 cases with shallow and 28 cases with silly hebephrenia.

At hospital admission there is rarely doubt about the schizophrenic character of the illness. Prognostically unfavourable items are more often coded, than in our total series of patients with schizophrenic outcome.

The two types of severe hebephrenic deterioration can be fairly well distinguished from each other in the chronic stages, but show very similar coded clinical characteristics at onset. Their coded symptoms resemble also those of the patients who develop slight hebephrenic deterioration.

Considering that slight hebephrenic deterioration is nearly twice as frequent as severe hebephrenic deterioration, one should be careful in predicting the latter outcome.

It also seems that modern treatment can prevent the development of severe hebephrenic deterioration to a large extent.

REFERENCES

1. Astrup, C. (1955) Untersuchungen mit der Assoziationsmethodik über Störungen im zweiten Signalsystem bei verschiedenen psychopathologischen Zuständen. Psychiat. Neurol. Med. Psychol. (Lpz.) 7, 326-334.

2. Astrup, C. (1959) The effects of ataraxic drugs on schizophrenic subgroups related to experimental findings. Acta psychiat. scand. Suppl. 136, 388-393.

3. Astrup, C. (1962) Schizophrenia: Conditional reflex studies. C. Thomas, Springfield, Ill.

4. Astrup, C. (1965) Long-term prognosis in functional psychoses with special regard to drug treatment. Bull. Assoc. Appl. Psychol. 75-79.

5. Astrup, C. (1969) Atypical paranoid schizophrenia. In Schizophrenie und Zyklothymie. (ed. G. Huber), Thieme, Stuttgart.

6. Astrup, C. & F. Fish (1964) The response of the different Leonhard subgroups of schizophrenia on psychotropic drugs. Fol. Psychiat. Neurol. Japon, 18, 133-140.

7. Astrup, C., A. Fossum & R. Holmboe (1959) A follow-up study of 270 patients with acute affective psychoses. Acta psychiat. scand. Suppl. 135.

8. Astrup, C., A. Fossum & R. Holmboe (1962) Prognosis in functional psychoses: Clinical, social and genetic aspects. C. Thomas, Springfield, Ill.

9. Astrup, C., A. Grimsgård, K. Helbnes, A. Kruse Jensen & M. Lid (1974) A study of flupenthixol decanoate and pipotiazine undecylenate in schizophrenics. Acta psychiat. scand. 50, 481-491.

10. Astrup, C., K. Håseth & P. Ofstad (1966) Prognostic models in functional psychoses based on studies of higher nervous activity. Activ. nervos. superior 8, 81-86.

11. Astrup, C. & K. Noreik (1966) Functional psychoses. Diagnostic and prognostic models. C. Thomas, Springfield, Ill.

12. Astrup, C. & K. Noreik (1970) The reliability of symptoms coding in functional psychoses. Acta psychiat. scand. 46, Suppl. 219, 18-25.

13. Austad, C. & Ø. Ødegård (1956) Gaustad Hospital through hundred years (Nor.), Oslo.

14. Basit, A. (1972) An investigation of Leonhard's classification of chronic schizophrenia.

15. Bleuler, M. (1941) Krankheitsverlauf, Persönlichkeit under Verwandtschaft Schizophrener und ihre gegenseitigen Beziehungen, Leipzig.

16. Bleuler, M. (1972) Schizophrene Verläufe im Lichte langjähriger Kranken-
    geschichten. Thieme, Stuttgart.

17. Bremer, J. (1951) A social psychiatric investigation of a small commun-
    ity in Northern Norway. Acta psychiat. (Kbh.) Suppl. 62.

18. Coderch, J., J.M. Costa Molinari & A.M. Sarró (1957) Contribución al
    estudio de la concepción pluralista de la esquizofrenia. Rev. psiquiat.
    psicol. méd. 5, 137-157.

19. Dalgard, O.S., & K. Noreik (1966) A study of psychopathy and their later
    development (Nor.) Nord. T. Krim. 76-94.

20. Evensen, H. (1904) Dementia praecox (Nor.), Oslo.

21. Evensen, H. (1936) Recherches, faites après la sortie sur env. 800 cas
    de démence précoce, traités a l'asile d'aliénés de Gaustad, durant les
    années 1915-19. Acta psychiat. (Kbh.) 11, 799-816.

22. Ey, H. (1958) Les problèmes cliniques des schizophrénies, Evolut.
    Psychiat. (Paris), 2, 148-211.

23. Ey, H. (1959) Unity and diversity of schizophrenia: Clinical and logical
    analysis of the concept of schizophrenia. Amer. J. Psychiat. 115, 706-714.

24. Faergeman, P. (1963) Psychogenic Psychoses. London.

25. Fischer, M. (1973) Genetic and environmental factors in schizophrenia.
    Munksgaard, Copenhagen.

26. Fish, F.J. (1958a) A clinical investigation of chronic schizophrenia.
    J. Ment. Sci. 104, 34-54.

27. Fish, F.J. (1958b) Leonhard's classification of schizophrenia. J.Ment.
    Sci. 104, 943-971.

28. Fish, F.J. (1962) Schizophrenia. Wright, Bristol.

29. Fish, F.J. (1964a) The influence of the tranquilizers on the Leonhard
    schizophrenic syndromes. L'Encéphale 1, 245-249.

30. Fish, F.J. (1964b) A guide to the Leonhard classification of chronic
    schizophrenia. Psychiat. Quart. 38, 1-13.

31. Fish, F. & C. Astrup (1964) The classification of chronic schizophrenia.
    A follow-up study. Fol. Psychiat. Neurol. Japon, 18, 17-23.

32. Flekkøy, K. & C. Astrup (1975) Prolonged clinical and experimental
    follow-up of hospitalized schizophrenics. Neuropsychobiol. 1, 47-58.

33. Gantt, W.H. (1962) Factors involved in the deveolment of pathological
    behavior: Schizokinesis and autokinesis. Perspect. Biol. Med. 5, 473-
    482.

34. Hirsch, S.R. & M. Shepherd (1974) Themes and variations in European
    psychiatry. Wright, Bristol.

35. Hoch, P.G., J.P. Cattell, M.O. Strahl and H.H. Pennes (1962) The
    course and outcome of pseudoneurotic schizophrenia. Amer. J. Psychiat.,
    119, 106-115.

36. Holmboe, R. & C. Astrup (1957) A follow-up study of 255 patients with
    acute schizophrenia and schizophreniform psychoses. Acta psychiat.
    scand. Suppl. 115.

37. Holmboe, R. , K. Noreik & C. Astrup (1968) Follow-up of functional psychoses at two Norwegian mental hospitals. Acta psychiat. scand. 44, 298-310.

38. Huber, G. (1966) Reine Defektsyndrome und Basisstadien endogener Psychosen. Fortschr. Neurol. Psychiat. 34, 409-421.

39. Janzarik, W. (1961) Die Typologie schizophrener Psychosen im Lichte der Verlaufsbetrachtung. Arch. Psychiat. 202, 140-154.

40. Janzarik, W. (1969) Nosographie und Einheitspsychose. In Schizophrenie und Zyklothymie. Huber, F. (ed.) Thieme, Stuttgart.

41. Jaspers, K. (1948) Allgemeine Psychopathologie. Berlin and Heidelberg.

42. Kleist, K. & W. Driest (1937) Die Katatonie auf Grund katamnestischer Untersuchungen. 1 Teil. Die als Katatonien verkannten Degenerationspsychosen. Z. ges. Neurol. Psychiat. 157, 479-556.

43. Kleist, K. , K. Leonhard & H. Schwab (1940) Die Katatonie auf Grund katamnestischer Untersuchungen. 3. Teil. Formen und Verläufe der eigentlichen Katatonie. Z. ges. Neurol. Psychiat. 168, 535-586.

44. Kleist, K. (1957) The symptoms of the different forms of schizophrenia within the scope of cerebral pathology. 2. Cong. Psychiat. Zürich.

45. Kleist, K. , K. Leonhard & E. Faust (1951) Die Hebephrenien auf Grund von katamnestischen Untersuchungen. Teil 2. Arch. Psychiat. Nervenkr. 186, 773-798.

46. Kleist, K. & H. Schwab (1950) Die verworrenen Schizophrenien auf Grund katamnestischer Untersuchungen. Teil 2. Die denkverwirrten Schizophrenien. Arch. Psychiat. Nervenkr. 184, 28-79.

47. Kraepelin, E. (1910) Psychiatrie. 8 Aufl. Leipzig.

48. Kretschmer, E. (1927) Der sensitive Beziehungswahn. 2. Aufl. Berlin.

49. Kringlen, E. (1964) Schizophrenia in male monozygotic twins. Acta psychiat. scand. Suppl. 178.

50. Kringlen, E. (1967) Heredity and environment in functional psychosis. Heinemann, London & Universitetsforlaget, Oslo.

51. Langfeldt, G. (1937) The prognosis of schizophrenia and the factors influencing the course of the disease. Copenhagen.

52. Langeldt, G. (1939) The schizophreniform states. Copenhagen.

53. Langfeldt, G. (1960) Diagnosis and prognosis of schizophrenia. Proc. Roy. Soc. Med. , 53, 1047-1052.

54. Leonhard, K. (1936) Die Defektschizophrenen Krankheitsbilder. Leipzig.

55. Leonhard, K. (1961) Die Spielbreite der unsystematischen Schizophrenien, besonders der Kataphasie. Arch. Psychiat. 202, 513-526.

56. Leonhard, K. (1966) Aufteilung der endogenen Psychosen. 3 Aufl. Akademie Verlag, Berlin.

57. Leonhard, K. (1969) Diagnose der Schizophrenie in verschiedenen Verläufsformen. Lebensversicherungsmedizin 21, 73-78.

58. Matussek, P. , A. Halbach & U. Troeger (1965) Endogene Depression. München and Berlin, Urban and Schwarzenberg.

59. Mauz, F. (1930) Die Prognostik der endogenen Psychosen. Leipzig.

60. Mitsuda, H. (1967) Clinical genetics in psychiatry. Bunko-sha, Kyoto.

61. Noreik, K. (1966a) Followed-up alcohol psychoses. (Nor.) Nord. psychiat. T. 20, 37-53.

62. Noreik, K. (1966 b) Followed-up organic psychoses. (Nor.) Nord. Med. 75, 69-73.

63. Noreik, K. (1970 a) Follow-up and classification of functional psychoses with special reference to reactive psychoses. Universitetsforlaget, Oslo.

64. Noreik, K. (1970 b) A follow-up examination of neuroses. Acta psychiat. scand. 46, 81-95.

65. Noreik, K. (1972) Psychoses associated with mental defiency. (Nor.) Nord. psychiat. T. 26, 288-295.

66. Noreik, K., C. Astrup, O.S. Dalgard & R. Holmboe (1967) A prolonged follow-up of acute schizophrenic and schizophreniform psychoses. Acta psychiat. scand. 43, 432-443.

67. Pauleikhoff, B. (1966) Die paranoid-halluzinatorische Psychose im 4. Lebensjahrzehnt. Fortschr. Neurol. Psychiat. 34, 548-560.

68. Perris, C. (1966) A study of bipolar (manic-depressive) and unipolar recurrent depressive psychoses. Acta psychiat. scand. Suppl. 194.

69. Retterstøl, N. (1966) Paranoid and paranoiac psychoses. Universitets-forlaget, Oslo.

70. Retterstøl, N. (1970) Prognosis in paranoid psychoses. Universitets-forlaget, Oslo.

71. Rosenthal, D. & S.S. Kety (1968) The transmission of schizophrenia. Pergamon, Oxford.

72. Roth, M. (1960 Depressive states and their borderlands: Classification, diagnosis and treatment. Comprehens. Psychiat. 1, 135-155.

73. Sarro Burbano, R. (1959) Desmembración de la esquizofrénia. II. Internat. Cong. Psychiat. Zürich, 310-311.

74. Schneider, F.W. (1955) Klinisch-katamnestische Untersuchungen an Schizophrenen eines Nervenlazaretten des Zweiten Weltkrieges. Schweiz. Arch. Neurol. Psychiat. 75, 227-272.

75. Schulz, B. & K. Leonhard (1940) Erbbiologisch-klinische Untersuchungen an insgesamt 99 im Sinne Leonhards typischen bzw. atypischen Schizophrenien. Z. ges. Neurol. Psychiat. 168, 587-613.

76. Schwab, H. (1938) Die Katatonie auf Grund katamnestischer Untersuchungen. 2. Teil. Die Erblichkeit der eigentlichen Katatonie. Z. ges. Neurol. Psychiat. 163, 441-506.

77. Schwab, H. (1942) Die paranoiden Schizophrenien auf Grund katamnestischer Untersuchungen. 2. Teil. Phantasieophrenie und progressive Konfabulose. Z. ges. Neurol. Psychiat. 173, 38-108.

78. Schwab, H. (1949) Die verworrenen Schizophrenien auf Grund katamnestischer Untersuchungen. 1. Teil. Die Schizophasien. Arch. Psyciat. Nervenkr. 182, 333-399.

79. Slater, E. (1953) Psychotic and neurotic illnesses in twins. Her Majesty's Stationary Office, London.

80. Slater, E., (A.W.) Beard & E. Glithers (1965) The schizophrenic-like psychoses of epilepsy. Internat. J. Psychiat. 1, 6-30.

81. Snezhnevsky, A.F. (1972) Schizophrenia: Multidisciplinary studies. (Rus.) Meditsina, Moscow.

82. Stein, C., Schulte von der (1955) Nachprüfung der Kleist-Leonhardsen Schizophrenieformen in den Frauenabteilungen einer Heil- und Pflegenanstalt. Arch. Psychiat. Nervenkr. 193, 303-336.

83. Storm-Mathisen, A. (1969) General paresis: A follow-up study of 203 patients. Acta psychiat. scand. 45, 118-132.

84. Tienari, P. (1963) Psychiatric illness in identical twins. Acta psychiat. scand. Suppl. 171.

85. Wernicke, C. (1906) Grundriss der Psychiatrie. 2. Aufl. Thieme, Leipzig.

86. Wing, J.K. & A.R. Hailey (1972) Evaluating a community psychiatric service. Oxford Un. Press, London.

87. Ødegard, Ø. (1967) Changes in the prognosis of functional psychoses since the days of Kraepelin. Brit. J. Psychiat. 113, 813-822.

88. Ødegard, Ø. (1972) The multifactorial theory of inheritance in predisposition to schizophrenia. In Kaplan, A.R., Genetic factors in schizophrenia. Thomas, Springfield, Ill.